NO BAD WAVES

TALKING STORY WITH MICKEY MUÑOZ

No Bad Waves - Talking Story With Mickey Muñoz
copyright 2011 Patagonia Books
Text © Mickey Muñoz
Foreword © Yvon Chouinard

Patagonia Books, Patagonia Inc.
259 W. Santa Clara St.
Ventura, CA 93001-2717.

First edition   Printed in Hong Kong on 100% recycled paper.

Patagonia Books, an imprint of Patagonia Inc., publishes a select
number of titles on wilderness, wildlife, and outdoor sports that
inspire and restore a connection to the natural world.

Editor - John Dutton
Photo Editor - Jeff Divine
Designer - Peter McBride
Production - Rafael Dunn
Project Management - Jennifer Sullivan

Front cover: John Severson

End papers: (front) Don James (back) Jeff Devine

ISBN 978-0-9801227-0-1 (regular edition)
ISBN 978-0-9801227-2-5 (boxed edition)

A Library of Congress number has been requested for this title.

There are no bad waves, only a poor choice
of equipment and a lousy attitude.

A wave is universal energy, changing in
response to environment and circumstance.

Any wave can be ridden if you combine
the right tools with body and spirit.

Matching the board to the wave
lets you flow instead of fight.

Attitude is the ultimate piece of equipment - no
matter how good the wave or how tuned the board
- a lousy attitude definitely ruins your day.

Surfing is dynamic and constantly changing:
Flow with the power and dance with wave.

- Mickey Muñoz

Table of Contents

Yvon Chouinard. *Mickey Muñoz*

Foreword
by Yvon Chouinard

In 1957, six young men made surfing history by being the first to ride the giant waves at Waimea on the North Shore of O'ahu. One of them, Pat Curren, went on to father the World Champion, Tom Curren. Another of them was Greg "Da Bull" Noll. People who were there can't remember whether Harry Church or Greg Noll caught the first wave, but without doubt, a young kid from California by the name of Mickey Muñoz caught the second wave.

Mickey does not look like he's a big-wave rider. He's my size – only 5 feet 4 inches tall and about 130 pounds. Since then, Mickey has become one of the greatest all-around water sportsmen in history. He is an excellent skin diver, fisherman, multi-hulled boat sailor. He also skis and snowboards. Mickey surfs every day there is swell and makes his living shaping some of the best surfboards in the world.

Like me, Mickey believes in never putting more than 75 percent into any endeavor. He would rather become proficient at a multitude of sports than become an expert at one.

For a while in my climbing career, I specialized at climbing only cracks; then I climbed only big walls; then I specialized in ice climbing and, eventually, Himalayan peaks. When I felt satisfied with my abilities, I would move on to another aspect of the sport or maybe even into another sport altogether. Mickey takes the same approach, but he has been involved in surfing since before the shortboard revolution, pioneered multihull design

and sailing, and dabbled in everything from stunt doubling to underwater demolition work to designing soapbox racers to wrestling bears.

I took a surfing trip to Indonesia with Mickey where we surfed some of the most exciting and dangerous waves either of us had experienced. On the last day of the trip, at Desert Point on the island of Lombok, I took off on the first wave of what turned out to be the largest set of the day. It was one of my best waves of the trip. I slid in and out of the tube twice before I finally punched out just before the curl crashed onto the reef. Bad mistake!

I tried to paddle outside before the next, and larger, wave caught me. No luck! That 3-meter wave broke on my head and snapped my board into three pieces. The next wave was even bigger, and Mickey was *on it*! He was completely locked into the tube, racing for his life. He passed between the reef and me, and went for another 75 meters before kicking out.

Here are Mickey's words about that ride: "The sound of the water sucking off the reef, roaring as it sweeps down hundreds of yards of coral shelf, draws you into the eye. Time becomes timeless, as if faster than light. You emerge younger, mindless, uncluttered – like a child laughing with stoke! Hooting! Hooting! Hooting! *A-w-w-w-o-o-o-o*!"

Today, Mickey is just as stoked as ever to surf, shape, boat, dive, or just hang out on the water. What follows is a selection of his stories.

Get Out There and Ride Those Waves

There was an advertisement that had a small guy in a beach chair sitting in the sand next to his date. Up comes a big muscular guy who kicks the chair over and kicks sand all over the little guy and takes the girl. Well, that was me; I was the weak little kid.

My mom was very conservative by nature, and in reality I was fairly conservative myself in my early years when we first came to the West Coast. Then I met Ricky Grigg, and he changed everything.

We moved from the East to the West Coast in 1943 into a house a couple blocks from the beach. My mom was athletic, and she enrolled me in swimming lessons at an early age and got me into competitive swimming. That's where I met Ricky and we became friends; we were both in the third grade and were in competitive swimming together.

Cub Scout Den 2 on parade. That's me second row back on the right, with Ricky Grigg right in front of me. The shorts we're wearing are all the same length, on me though they came down below my knees. Santa Monica. *Mickey Muñoz Collection*

Ricky lived on the beach just south of the Santa Monica Pier at Gorilla Park, it was called that because that's where all the weight lifters hung out – Muscle Beach. He bodysurfed, belly-boarded, and rode air mats at Santa Monica and Will Rogers state beaches.

Ricky started board surfing a little bit before I did, and he got me into surfing and then into progressively bigger and bigger waves. Ricky would intimidate me and scold me into the surf: "You asshole, get out there; get out there and ride those waves."

I eventually bought a Surf King Junior, which was a kook box, a lifeguard hollow paddleboard. The same company made the Surf King Senior and the Surf King Junior. The Senior was 12' long; the Junior was 10'6". It weighed just about what I did at the time – about 65 pounds – and I could just barely drag it to the water.

After surfing, I was too tired to drag it out of the water, so I would have to end-for-end it to get it back up the beach. The lifeguards at State Beach let me keep the board in their station when I couldn't get it home. This was in 1947 and 1948. The board was an awkward surfing vehicle. Like Ricky, I bodysurfed and rode surf mats and belly boards. When I got that 10'6" paddleboard, I started to ride 1-foot waves inside the Santa Monica breakwater.

In the winter of 1950, I conned my mom into loaning me money to buy a new surfboard. I bought a brand-new Joe Quigg board that Joe had made for his wife, Aggie. It was 8'10" long, 24" wide, with a 16" tail block, and a very light – for the time – balsa board. That was my first real surfboard.

I have loved Joe's approach to design ever since. He is a dedicated waterman who has spent a long life thinking about design – a long life filled with intelligence and artfulness. And all along, Ricky was pushing me and pushing my conservative nature, encouraging me to ride bigger and bigger waves.

Mom took this shot of me at Malibu in 1950, when I was 13, riding my first real surfboard, an 8'10" Joe Quigg shape. *Virginia Muñoz*

The Uplifters Ranch
and Early Santa Monica

We lived in that house in Ocean Park for about a year, and then my parents found a house up in the Uplifters Ranch, which at the turn of the century used to be called the Cuplifters Ranch. It was an escape from the city for movie people, artists, and the well-to-do. It was in the wedge formed by Santa Monica Canyon, Coast Highway, and Sunset, just above the canyon.

It was the beach escape from the city of Los Angeles before Malibu was built up. It's hard to believe, but that section of Santa Monica was once out in the country. When we moved there, it was all dirt roads. We lived in a seven-bedroom, all-redwood house on an acre of land; the whole Uplifters Ranch was probably 500 acres or more. There was a country club with an Olympic-sized swimming pool, tennis courts, an outdoor theater, horse stables, and a polo grounds. Johnny Weissmuller, the first "Tarzan," lived across the street. Earl Warren – the future governor of California and later Chief Justice of the Supreme Court – and his kids lived just up the street.

My sister had horses, there were creeks and woods, and we were walking distance to the beach. I went to Canyon School, which consisted of an old church building and a couple of one-room buildings. There were maybe 50 kids in the whole school. We could go to school barefooted, and I would walk or ride my bike to school. It was pretty loose – and pretty fine.

School totally lost me by sixth grade. I was a pretty good student, but then surfing got me. I kept going to school because I was interested in learning, but except for a few classes, I was bored with it.

Will Rogers State Beach was right at the mouth of the canyon. I grew up on that beach. We used to swim at the Jonathan Club located on the Coast Highway between Will Rogers State Beach and Santa Monica Pier. That was my territory growing up and where I got initiated into the ocean.

There were some very famous bars in Santa Monica: lots of gay people, movie people, artists – all living alternative lifestyles. I saw Gerry Mulligan on more than one occasion come out of the parking lot at the Sip 'n' Surf blowing his horn and Ray Brown playing his stand-up bass and Richie Kamuca – some of the world's best jazz musicians of the time played there.

I worked for Pat Dorian who owned the Sip 'n' Surf. He was a big influence in my early years. I worked in his restaurant, bussing and washing dishes. When I turned 21 years old, I learned to tend bar. Pat took me under his wing, and we stayed friends through the years.

I remember grabbing your privates was always part of the noseriding experience – a part of the noseriding put-on. *Bud Browne*

Tommy Zhan (l) and Joe Quigg (r) flank a trophy board Joe shaped in the late '40s; both were exceptional paddlers and surfers. The template, with a pointy nose and pulled-in tail, wouldn't be out of place today.
Joe Quigg Collection

Pure Luck

Humans gravitate toward structure, but surfing isn't very structured. No matter how much you plan it, once you get in the water and paddle out, all bets are off. The ocean is in constant flux, and the act of riding a wave is a spontaneous, creative exercise. You either like that or you don't, and at least in the early days it attracted an eclectic group of characters – unusual, nonconservative people who didn't value structure.

You also had to be physically fit to be capable of surfing. I got in at the end of the 100-pound board era. I was little and light and couldn't have lifted a 100-pound board – again timing was everything. I just happened to luck into that real light balsa board that Joe had made for Aggie. Otherwise, I may not have continued surfing. It was pure luck that I became a surfer.

In the late 1940s and early 1950s – after the war when things had quieted down a bit – there were only a few pockets of surfing along the coast: La Jolla, San Onofre and Dana Point, in the Santa Monica and Malibu area, and Santa Cruz. Lucky for me, I grew up in one of those pockets of surfing. It also happened that two of the premiere shapers of the time, Matt Kivlin and Joe Quigg, lived in the area that I grew up.

Added to that, I was exposed to some of the more progressive surfboard designs because our local wave, Malibu, was one of the most consistently shaped waves known in the surfing world at the time. A rider could experiment on that wave, and surfboard designs progressed fast. The wave itself was conducive to evolving one's surfing. Because of the close proximity of the aircraft industry and the technological developments from the war, we were the first area to incorporate fiberglass into building surfboards. Then we started traveling up to Rincon, another great point wave, and another door was opened.

Early Influences

There weren't any formal board manufacturers back then. If you wanted a board, you had to know somebody. Quigg and Kivlin were shaping boards for themselves and their friends, and I got to know them through working for them. One of my first jobs in the surf industry was basically performing the duty of a paperweight.

Quigg or Kivlin would shape a board on the beach at Malibu using adzes to rough shape the balsa planks, then drawknives and planes to finish it. They would first put the blank on the sand and stand on it and use the adze to rough shape the blank. When it came to the drawknife, there was a lot of resistance, and they couldn't stand on the board and use the drawknife. They needed somebody to sit on the board and hold it down, so that became my first job in the surfboard business: a paperweight. My pay at day's end was a quart of beer: We would talk story around a balsa-chip fire and share that quart of beer.

Watching Quigg and Kivlin shape those boards spawned my interest in surfboard design and shaping – especially Quigg being the craftsman that he was. It was fascinating to me.

I got other jobs in the surf industry: sweeping floors at Velzy's and sanding surfboards in an open lot in Venice for Alan Gomes, who was glassing Dale Velzy and Jacobs boards. I also ran the gamut of the restaurant business: washing pots and pans, scrubbing floors and dishes, bussing and then waiting tables, and finally learning to bartend.

I grew up around people interested in the water, in surfing, and in shaping surfboards. A lot of them had taken jobs as lifeguards and so were exposed to a lot of different facets of water knowledge. They had to know boats, they had to know dories, swimming, paddling, waves . . . .

I knew Phil Edwards by reputation only. My mom had taken our family camping down south of Oceanside. We had our surfboards with us, and we camped behind the lagoon. To get to the surf, we paddled across the lagoon and then walked across the beach.

I paddled out at this little pointbreak called Guayule Point, which was Phil's break – his nickname was the Guayule Kid – and there was Phil. He took off on a wave as I paddled out; he made a turn, got his board in trim, walked up on his board and his tail slid out and he side-slipped in the wave. Then he casually and smoothly stepped back, reset the fin, and went on down the line as I pushed through the wave. That just totally dazzled me, and he's dazzled me ever since with his boat and board designs and his ethics. He was a very powerful and very smooth surfer with terrific wave judgment and an ability to read the water.

Pete Peterson was around when I was young, and he was considered if not the best, then among the best, all-around watermen in the world. I got to hang out with Pete a bit: surfing, diving, and being on boats with him. He influenced me a lot just through that contact.

OPPOSITE TOP:
Wayne Shafer, Harrison Ealy, and Phil Edwards on Flippy's first boat – a P-Cat with an outboard on it – heading down to Church to test out noseriding prototypes. San Clemente. *Mickey Muñoz*

OPPOSITE BOTTOM:
Phil Edwards, after a go-out at Poche, walks past the Tahitian shack that Wayne Shafer built right on the beach, complete with board rack and outdoor bar. *Mickey Muñoz*

Malibu Rocketeering

Miki Dora came to Malibu after I had been surfing there a while. He was a pretty good scammer, so he fit right in with the Hollywood Malibu crowd. Dora was such a better surfer than 99 percent of the surfers at Malibu because at the time he showed up, there was a big influx of people from the San Fernando Valley who came over and tried to learn to surf. There was a big difference between the really good surfers and the not-so-good surfers. And Dora had style. He just had this flair about him.

Miki and I got into rocketeering – making model rockets. We had to go to Tijuana to get some of the ingredients that we couldn't get north of the border. Miki made this rocket out of a 6-foot long piece of metal tubing, and he shaped a nose cone for it. It was just after the Russians had done their first space trip, so he shaped this sputnik to go on the tip of the rocket. It had the fins and the whole thing.

We went to Malibu to launch it. It was wintertime, there wasn't any surf, and no one was on the beach. We built a launch tower for the rocket and dug a bunker in the sand to hide behind. We wore lab coats that we had found, and carefully measured out all the ingredients that Dora had brought along inside a briefcase. We mixed up this pretty dangerous stuff and tamped it down inside the rocket. The guy we picked to light the fuse had broken his leg and was on crutches. We had photographers, and by the time we were ready to light the rocket, more people had accumulated. We sent this guy out on his crutches in the sand to light the fuse, and then he hobbled back and dove into the bunker.

The rocket didn't go up; it went out – in lots of pieces. It broke windows on the pier, and it rattled a cop car with a policeman asleep inside, parked south of the pier. He woke up and came poking around. Meanwhile of course, we had cleaned up as much of the evidence as we could.

Down the beach came the cop with a little kid in tow. In the cop's hand was this twisted, smoldering piece of metal. We were down behind the bunker talking story when he came up, and the kid pointed at us as the culprits. In a stern voice the cop asked, "All right, who are the rocketeers?"

Dora replied, "Racketeers? Racketeers? There are no racketeers here." Then Dora went through a whole song and dance with the cop.

Finally, the cop just smiled and said, "No more rockets."

Rocket scientists at work in Malibu.
Mickey Muñoz Collection

Another early Malibu story involved me, Bobby Patterson, and a friend of ours, Charlie Riemers. They were both older than me and had their driver's licenses. Charlie was kind of a cheapskate, and we would have to pony up for gas every time he drove, which is probably how it should have been.

One night we were in Malibu, sleeping on the beach. We had a campfire going and were drinking a bottle of wine; we got pretty out there, and Charlie passed out. Bobby, seizing the opportunity, said, "You know, let's get Charlie. Let's burn his board."

I objected, "I don't know. Jeez, that's not too good an idea."

"No, no, come on, let's burn his board. You know, that asshole, remember . . ." and he rambled off on a drunken rant. Bobby grabbed what he thought was Charlie's board and threw it on the fire. The balsa board started to burn, and the fiberglass made an awful stink. Charlie was passed out under his

sleeping bag, and the board was smoldering on the fire. Luckily, the board put the fire out. I don't remember whether Bobby or I pulled the board out of the fire and threw sand on it. Soon everybody was passed out.

The next morning the surf was really good, so we got ready to surf a dawn patrol. Bobby looked for his board and started to panic. "Where's my board? Where's my board?"

Charlie was already paddling out. While Bobby was still looking for his board, I grabbed my board and snuck out behind him to the surf. We left Bobby on the beach. He had thrown his own board into the fire.

ABOVE:
Me, Miki Dora, and Mike Doyle performing the unusual "trandum." Malibu. *John Severson*

19

The Hawaiian Influence

Bobby Patterson came over to the mainland while my family was still living in the Uplifters Ranch in the early '50s. Joe Quigg and Matt Kivlin had gone to Hawai'i and met Bobby. He was considered the best small wave rider in Hawai'i – and possibly the world – at that time. Matt invited him to come to California and stay with him. Matt introduced us, and Bobby and I started surfing together and became inseparable pals. Bobby was a little older and had his driver's license. I was months away from getting my driver's license at 14 when they changed the age up to 16. Bobby's license solved a lot of our travel problems for surfing.

After some time, Bobby felt like he was getting close to over-staying his welcome at Matt's, who at the time was getting married. I invited him to stay with my family. We had a big house at Uplifters. I had my own room with my own entrance and bathroom, almost like my own apartment. Bobby became part of the family.

About that time one of Duke's nephews, Bunny Kahanamoku, was hanging out at State Beach. There were a lot of Hawaiians who had gravitated to Santa Monica, and I knew a bunch of them. Bobby, being Hawaiian – born and raised in Manoa Valley – naturally fit in with these other Hawaiian guys. That was our crew of friends; we all surfed and partied together.

Like everyone else I wanted to go to Hawai'i. It was pretty expensive dollar for dollar compared to today's prices, and my parents weren't going to finance it, so I had to scrape up the money myself.

I learned how to use resin and fiberglass, and I repaired boards in my family garage. Miki Dora and I would smoke cigars, drink gin, and repair boards. After my grandfather died, he left hundreds of boxes of cigars stacked up in our garage; we would crack open one of those boxes. My dad had his gin stash there too, so we would open a gin bottle and pour off a bit of gin

Bobby Patterson, arguably one of the best surfer's at the time, in Santa Barbara. *John Severson*

and replace it with water, so it looked like it hadn't been touched. That watered gin probably prolonged my father's life a little. We would drink the gin with lemonade, smoke the cigars, listen to Chico Sesma, and repair boards.

I repaired some boards, sold a bike, and managed to scrape together $125 for a one-way ticket for my first trip to Hawai'i in 1954 with Dora, Mike Donahue, and Jimmy Fisher. I landed with $6 in my pocket on a one-way ticket, and I had to find a job right away. I ended up working for a restaurant called the Embers, bussing tables and washing dishes. Jimmy Fisher and Dora pretty much were shoplifters and scammers. I would go out on their forays sometimes to see how they operated and did a little bit of it myself.

While I was there, Bobby wanted me to meet his brother Raymond. As soon as I got there, I went for a surf at Waikiki. When I got out of the water, I was carrying my board up Liliuokalani Avenue, and up behind me came a lowered Mercury with four guys sitting so low that you could just see their eyes over the windows.

"Oh, geez," I thought, "what's this?" Out came Raymond with a big smile on his face, and a 'ukulele in his hands. I never saw Raymond put his 'ukulele down from that time till he died – he was phenomenal. He was probably one of the best 'ukulele players in Hawai'i, and a good surfer too.

I rode Waikiki mostly but took a trip around the island to ride other places as well. I didn't stand-up ride at Sunset, although it was a 4- to 5-foot day, but I did bodysurf it. My dad finally talked me into coming home after living that summer in Hawai'i; he paid my way back so I could go to school.

The Early
Shaping Business

In the big, heavy board days, you would take off and trim across the wave. Sometimes you would get ahead of the curl, and there were stalling maneuvers like stepping back on the tail of the board to break its trim and slow it down. The curl would catch up with you, and then you would re-establish trim and go ahead. They were big, heavy boards, but we developed the skills to not only stall them in a straight line but also got them to turn a bit.

Then as the boards got lighter and the bottoms got more progressive, they planed a little faster and turned easier and more abruptly. The fin had been in use for a while. The fin designs depended on where they were placed and the size of the fins, and that of course affected board performance.

We were learning all of this at Malibu – this beautiful mechanical wave – that was uncrowded at that time. We were able to stay in the water for six to eight hours a day. It was the ideal place to evolve surfing performance and surfboard design. We were catching literally hundreds and hundreds of waves a day and were able to replicate maneuver after maneuver on wave after wave. We, a group of young kids, pushed each other into more radical maneuvers and more radical surfing all the time.

Bobby Patterson would be out surfing and Dewey Weber would come up from Manhattan Beach and would go out too and start pushing Bobby. Bobby was a huge influence on my surfing. We were both physically small – an advantage at Malibu, which didn't get big that often – and tended to ride smaller, more maneuverable boards that fit in the waves better than the bigger boards. We were young and didn't care about how we looked. We were just out there hooting and laughing and having fun.

Joe Quigg's surfing and design were a little more conservative, but his genius was his ability to condense the extremes. An example, and one of Joe's exercises that impressed me, was he took all the hot sailboat designs of the day – the long narrow skinny ones that did well to weather and the short fat ones that did well downwind – and he drew them in proportion on the same sheet of graph paper. He superimposed them on each other until he came out with an average of all the different hulls.

That's how Quigg designed most of his boards. That's why he was the genius shaper he was: He could go out on the end of the pendulum swing of design and then bring it back to the middle, deviating only slightly one way or the other for the personality of the person he was shaping the board for.

A few people got into the surfboard-making business. Quigg got into it because it was a way to make a living, to survive, while surfing and designing boats. It was a way to make a living, or try to make a living, and also to advance your surfing. As more people got into it, Dale Velzy started to turn a profit by making boards. But it has never been that profitable an industry.

Bob Simmons was kind of on his own design tangent, and his designs were actually very progressive. Obviously, he was making up for his physical disabilities. He hurt his arm in a bicycle accident and couldn't paddle that well. He wasn't a great swimmer or waterman, and he wasn't physically endowed. He made boards that paddled faster, were more stable, and trimmed faster, especially on bigger waves. He was a ballsy guy and could ride big waves. He pushed himself and his equipment. He also had some sort of formal aerodynamic training and engineering background. He designed boards like airplane wings to have more lift and have less drag.

I shaped my first balsa board for myself in the mid-1950s. That ended up as the proverbial toothpick syndrome: I started big and ended small; I didn't know what I was doing. I ended up with this pretty radical, thin, narrow 7'6'' board. I rode it for a while and then gave it to Ronald Patterson, Bobby's other brother, who was a really good surfer at the time. Both Ronald and Bobby rode it and really liked it.

At the same time, I was dabbling in working for Velzy and then eventually for Hobie where I learned production surfboard manufacturing. Hobie hired me to repair and patch boards; then I learned to glass in a production environment. I learned to make fins and to glass on fins and all the facets of glassing, glossing, sanding, hot coating, pin lining, . . . all of that. Then I started shaping in production and learned to shape. Ralph Parker was one of my original teachers who taught me the system for shaping – how to do a production board.

The Hobie factory at that time was building complete surfboards from start to finish. We weren't just shaping them and sending them to a glasser; we were doing everything. The only thing we did not do was blow the foam. We cut the blanks, milled the wood, glued the wood into the blanks, made the fins, glassed the fins on or made the fin boxes glossed with resin, polished the boards, packed them, and shipped them. We could put out over 200 boards a week in our heyday.

There were seven or eight shapers, three glassers, at least one or two sanders, and three or four glossers and hot coaters. We had a guy who did nothing but mill wood and glue blanks. Hobie designed the tools to make it all happen. He was a genius engineer and designer. Don Walton also helped design and build tools to make the 200 boards per week production a reality. His nickname was "Dovetail" for good reason; he was an incredible craftsman and engineer. He didn't surf, and it was probably good for our production goals that he didn't.

Bobby Patterson was a glosser there and absolutely, anally meticulous about his brushes and his workspace. He wouldn't let anybody touch anything in his glossing room; he had his special way he cleaned his brushes. They had to be perfect, because to him glossing was an art. It was a dance. Bobby would smoke Pall Malls, and there'd be an ash about an inch or two long hanging off the end of his cigarette. Bobby would be running down these boards applying the resin with this ash sticking over these gleaming beauties. We would watch and wonder if the ash was going to fall into the fresh resin, but it never did.

Ronald Patterson smoked five packs of cigarettes a day. He couldn't sleep through the night; he would wake up and light the next cigarette with the burning filter of his last one. He was a sander, and his theory was as long as he had a filtered cigarette in his mouth and inhaled through the filter, he didn't need a mask to sand surfboards. He outlived his brothers, both Bobby and Raymond.

Part of the reason to get into all of that was, of course, to make a living, to be around the people you surf with and as a means to an end: The whole thing was about surfing. For me, it was easiest to be in the surfboard business to continue surfing. A bigger motivation to shape was that I had specific design ideas I wanted to try. I wanted to compliment whatever surfing ability I had and was designing boards to get me where I wanted to be in surfing.

Buzzy Trent's Commitment

Another one of my gurus was Buzzy Trent. Buzzy was a local Santa Monica guy, who went to Santa Monica High and was a football player there. He was physically endowed and a gutsy surfer; he rode as big a waves as anybody and as far back.

We went up to Rincon a lot in the winter at that time and also surfed Overhead. Overhead was the closest thing that we had to the hard-breaking outside waves in Hawai'i. Buzzy loved Overhead. He would take me there and paddle out with me and encourage me into waves. Buzzy would never take off in front of anybody. He was always farther inside, closer to the curl. That was just Buzzy's ethic, and he tried to instill that in me. He knew it was better to commit completely to the ride.

When you're surfing Pipeline, you need to commit totally. You're better off going for it than trying to pull back at the last second because the wipeouts when you pull back are way worse. You have to want it, and even though you've made a mistake and know you've taken off too late or you can't do it, you still need to go for it because it's worse if you don't.

You can apply that one to life in general. Don't be dumb. Don't think you can stand in front of a train or jump out of an airplane without a para-chute and flap your wings and fly. Don't be totally stupid, but if you do commit to something, go for it. You'll learn from the wipeouts. So you take off deeper in the pocket and you might not make a lot of waves, but the ones you do will be real rewards.

Me at Makaha Point Surf. Point Surf was always underrated as a big wave spot: I've gone as fast there as I've ever gone on a surfboard.
Leroy Grannis

Stunt Doubling

The *Gidget* movie came at the end of an era; it introduced surfing to a huge number of people. It was a double-edged sword, though. On the business side, it was good for people making surfboards, but it was bad for surfing because it led to crowded lineups.

Most of the women who surfed in that day were pretty good-sized women, and they hired Sandra Dee as the actress to play Gidget in that film, because Gidget was small, a girl midget. I knew the second unit director on the film, and he hired me to do some of the surfing for Sandra Dee. I put a bikini on, rode some waves, and got paid – not a bad deal. Through that, I made enough money and put in enough time to get into SAG – not an easy union to get into.

That SAG membership allowed me to get other stunt jobs, and I doubled for Mickey Rooney in a comedy TV series. He was good at stunts himself – he taught me some fight moves and fall techniques – but they couldn't afford to have him get hurt.

The highlight of the show was a water ski skit. I had never water skied in my life, so I got a friend of mine who had a ski boat to take me out one day for three or four hours. The stunt had me standing on a dock getting instruction from a woman ski instructor. The towline was coiled at my feet, and I had the tow bar in my hand. The line was connected to a boat idling off the dock.

As the instructor told me, the plan was for the guy in the boat to suddenly gun it and tow me off the dock. I would land in the water and end up on my back with my skis over my head. The woman ski instructor (who happened to be Marge Calhoun) was attached to the boat by another tow line and would get towed off the dock at the same time, and would land next to me and rescue me. I would grab her legs and pull myself onto the tail of her skis so we were then tandem waterskiing. I would then climb up her back to finish sitting on her shoulders in a tandem water ski routine. It was a comedy skit, but not so easy to do.

We tried to figure out how I was going to get towed on my back, and finally I decided to make a board – a piece of plywood shaped like a belly board – and strap it to my back under my shirt. I drilled a hole in the nose of the board, and attached the towline that went to the boat. I held a fake towline in my hands, because I wasn't strong enough to hold the actual towline long enough to get on a plane.

The first time we tried the stunt, I got towed off the dock, lost one ski and had to ski on a single ski. I pulled that off OK, and that part of the shot was in the bag. Towing me when I would spin around and fall on my back wasn't so easy. We needed a way to get me on a plane fast without going under water, so I got my surfboard, and I would start on the tail of my board on my back, the tow boat would get up to a speed that I would be able to plane at, then the boat driver would punch it, and I'd get towed off the board, land in the water, and off I would go.

That worked, at least for the first two or three times we tried it, but they wanted more shots. The next time we tried, instead of planing up I planed down to 20 feet underwater; the boat driver was looking forward concentrating on where he was going and never knew I was in trouble until the towline broke. Lucky for me it did, there was no way I could get to the line, no safety backup. A good lesson: Always have a backup plan! We should have had a safety person in the boat looking back all the time, but we didn't.

We ended up pulling it off, and they liked what we did. I guess Mickey liked me and asked me to do more shows, but unfortunately the series wasn't continued. If it had, that might have turned into a career for me; doubling Mickey Rooney would not have been bad.

Me and Bobby Patterson clowning around on a movie set at Poche.
Mickey Muñoz Collection

27

Skiing at Alta

The winter after I got back from my first trip to Hawai'i, Bobby, Rodney Shimmons, Jocko, and I got in my 1941 Cadillac and drove to Alta, Utah. We went to the Army Surplus Store and bought coat liners – ankle-length fur coats soldiers used to line their jackets with in the winter. You could carry an entire case of beer in the pockets. We took about a week and a half to get to Alta, stopping at every bar that we could find on the way. We made quite a scene when we got there. We had jobs lined up and worked that winter as ski bums.

I was a really shitty skier – terrible form – but I could get down almost anything, and because of surfing, I had no fear. I was a coordinated enough athlete to pull it off without the proper technique.

The first time I rode up the Germania lift at Alta, I was with a friend who was a ski instructor there. He pointed out the various runs you can see from the lift. On Baldy Peak there are two principal chutes, aptly named the Big Chute and the Little Chute. My ski instructor friend told me that the Big Chute had been run about eight or nine times, and the Little Chute only once. By today's standards, the average person could probably do them, but back then I looked at them and thought, "Oh my God, I can't believe anybody could even stick on the snow, much less be able to do that." That was my first day on the mountain, and what he told me haunted me.

I worked as a ski bum and had my work set up so that I could ski five days a week; all I wanted to do was ski. I also loved to climb the slopes and had gear to do that. When the lifts were down, I'd go hike and climb. I got to hang out with a guy by the name of Ed LaChapelle because I skied so much. He was considered the best snow ranger in the United States, if not the world, at the time.

Ed was the guy who monitored the slopes for avalanche danger, and I got to go up and check it out with him before the lifts opened. They had a cannon they could aim at the obvious places that were vulnerable to sliding, and early in the morning before the lifts were open – *Boom*, and then, *Crack* – they'd fire the gun and set off avalanches.

Then Ed would have to go in with the dynamite and blow up the spots they couldn't reach with the gun. By law, he wasn't allowed to carry both the dynamite and the caps; by common sense, you don't want to be up there alone, so he always had to have somebody with him. I got to be friends with him, and I loved to climb the slopes, so naturally I got to go with him and carry the caps. We would blow up these avalanche danger spots, and of course we would get the sacred first tracks. I skied places that you would never ski as a tourist.

Midway through the season, I ended up climbing Baldy and skiing the Big Chute. Then I made a date to ski the Little Chute with a guy named Jim McConkey. Jim snuck up there before we had planned to do the run and did it by himself. We got some light snowfall so Jim's tracks were gone, and I knew it was stable. I still wanted to do the run, so on my next lunch break at work, I told my boss in the kitchen my plan and to give me two and a half hours, "If I'm not back, maybe you better come and get me." He told me I was crazy.

It was about a 45-minute climb to the top of the hill and into the chute; it was pretty tricky getting in. I finally got positioned and made one turn and fell. Luckily the snow was just right and I didn't slide. I got up, side-stepped back up to the top and skied it nonstop all the way back down the whole hill. I guess I was the third person to ski it. Of course, now it's probably skied every day, but at that time, it was a big deal.

With knickers, hand-painted socks and a beret, I'm hoping to gain the European skiing maestros' skills by imitating their dress. *Fred K Lindholm*

Surfing sequence on the first day we rode Waimea in 1957.
Note that we were riding Malibu-style boards. *Don James*

Surfing Waimea
Made Me Bigger

The next time I went back to Hawai'i was in 1957 when we spent the whole winter on the North Shore and ended up surfing Waimea. That winter, I rode some big waves and came back with extreme confidence.

The group of us over there had talked about riding Waimea and had gone by to look at it. Waimea appeared to be the last place on the North Shore that was rideable when everywhere else was closed out. A bunch of us had gathered, and we were standing on the road to check it out. I can't remember who suggested we go out, but, "OK, let's do it!"

There were about seven or eight of us who went out on that morning. We waxed our boards and waited until we could get out through the shorebreak and then paddled out. There's controversy over who rode the first wave; I'm not so sure who it was. I was more concerned with sharks than I was with the waves at that particular time. I took off on a wave and saw one of the guys, who had taken off on the wave in front, inside with his arm over the side of his board. I went down the face of the wave, made it to the bottom and couldn't make the wave, so I proned out and had a death grip on my board and was headed right for him. I figured it was either me or him, so I held on and luckily I bounced over him and kept going. I managed to get out of the soup before the shorebreak and paddle back out again.

Relaxing after the morning surf: Greg Noll in the foreground, then me; behind is Bob Bermel and to the right, Mike Stang. Waimea Bay. *Mickey Muñoz Collection*

I didn't even realize how gnarly it was until I got back on shore after the session. We went in the water about 8:30 in the morning, and I got in around noon. I got back up on the beach and joined a bunch of people who were watching the surf. A set came, and I jumped up and down and yelled, "Gee, look at the size of that wave."

Somebody nearby said that I was in a lot of waves that big, that was an average set. It shocked me because when I was out there I didn't realize how big it was – I guess my adrenaline was pumping and I was caught up in the excitement of the whole thing.

It started to get blown out, and in the meantime someone on the beach opened up the Waimea river mouth with a tractor, which compounded the bad rip already there. Later that afternoon, Creg Noll had his camera and was filming, so he tried to pump Mike Stang and me to go out again, "Oh, you guys, you gotta go out, you gotta go out." So Mike and I paddled out. It had gotten bigger and gnarlier; the rip was really wild and there was a lot of bump on it.

Mike had taken a drama course in school where he had read a little Shakespeare, and I was into that stuff too. Mike with his long curly hair and bushlike beard started to quote Othello,

"I took by the throat the circumcised dog and smote him thus," and he fell off his board.

We were both screaming and wild-eyed, rain squalls were coming through, the conditions were gnarly, and then this huge set came up, and Mike and I both paddled for it. We took off on this giant wave after getting pumped up with Shakespeare's Othello. I think we both got wiped out, but what an experience.

Maybe that was a significant day in the history of surfing; at the time we didn't know it. In retrospect, though, after I got back from Hawai'i that winter, having ridden Waimea and Sunset, and after taking on whatever the North Shore offered, I felt bigger. Being small going through junior high school and high school is tough. You are always being compared to the football and basketball players. They seemed to get the best-looking girls. After that winter surfing in Hawai'i, my stature grew – at least in my own mind.

That winter also proved to me that if you put your mind to it and you think positive, you can do about anything you set your mind to. I realized that my only limitations were my own limited thinking. All I had to do was set my mind to doing a thing, put enough effort into it, and I could do it. That was a big leap of growth in my early life.

Frank Donahue and the Shark

Frank Donahue was an amazing character. I did some film work with him and got to hang out with him quite a bit. He was a ballsy, multitalented guy. Frank was a writer for the local Santa Monica paper, a screenwriter, a stuntman, a second unit director, a diver – the list goes on – and he was married to a gorgeous Hollywood starlet.

The Navy had dive tables that were reasonably conservative, but because of the riches in deep diving, people pushed the limits all the time, and a lot of people got hurt. Frank was one of those amazing people who didn't. He claimed he had done two deep jump dives to over 300 feet and got away with it. He went down to 300 feet on straight air – which is really pushing it – then held his breath and dove another 25 feet to do a job for an oil company. He had to reposition an oil-drilling rig. He made $1,000 a dive, huge money in those days.

Being an all-around water person, he did a shark fight once as a stuntman that involved a 12-foot tiger shark. Frank was 210 or 220 pounds, and he's got a picture of himself standing in the jaws of the tiger shark; that's how big it was.

Frank heard about a film being made that would need a shark-footage sequence, so he set out to shoot the sequence and sell it to the film company. Frank hired me to be the stunt double for a female and a male. Because I'm a small guy, I would make a small shark look bigger, and of course smaller sharks are easier to work with. It was in the spring, and the water wasn't exactly warm, probably high 50s. We were in a 25-foot powerboat towing another skiff behind. We motored out about five miles and started chumming to bring in the sharks.

While we were waiting for the sharks to come, Frank told shark stories: "You don't have to worry about blue sharks; you gotta carry the fight with them. They got small mouths and you can hardly get them to bite you. That's what we're gonna be catching is a blue shark. There's no problem with them; the gill slits are so small you can hardly get your hand in . . . " On and on he went about how easy it was going to be.

It got toward the end of the first day, and we hadn't caught a shark. We had a bunch of lines out – hands lines and some rods – and the skiff was out chumming. The sun was getting fairly low, and Frank was muttering about getting out of there as it was getting too late. Getting ready to leave, I started to pull in one of the hand lines and felt a weight on the end, "Jesus, I think I got something here."

Frank grabbed the line and hauled in a 7-foot shark. The shark turned out to be a mako, not a blue, and when we got it in the boat, the shark went nuts – tore up the gas lines, bit the transom, tore at the wood. "This is a gnarly shark," I thought.

Frank started screaming, "Get in your costume! Get in your costume!"

"What do you mean? This is no docile shark!" I screamed back.

"Get in your costume!" Frank insisted.

He was lying on the shark trying to subdue it. "Don't worry

about a thing. We can just hang him by the tail. It knocks them out." When they're hanging, their liver compresses their heart and slows down the heart-beats. It takes a little time to wake up if they're not moving forward.

"I don't know. This looks really bad," I replied as the wood chips and contents of the boat are flying through the air from the destruction this shark was inflicting. "You gotta at least sew the mouth shut." So Frank took some wire leader and sewed it shut.

The camera guy had a lot of experience; he was in a full wetsuit, had a lung on, and used a 35 mm camera in a big enclosure. He had some pretty good protection. Frank had a wetsuit and lung on. I was in a sarong, a hair-piece, and pancake makeup: I was feeling vulnerable. The three of us got in the water in a triangle with Frank who was holding onto the shark.

The plan was for Frank to throw the shark at me. "Don't let that fucker go. You gotta roll over on your back and as soon as you hear the camera shut off, you gotta get the shark, 'cause you're closest to it."

"You're kidding." I replied.

"No."

That was the first time I had ever seen a shark underwater. As soon as the shark got in the water, he opened his mouth and ripped out all the stitches. We all went underwater, and Frank threw the shark at me. I pushed it away, and as soon as I heard the camera switch off, I swam after it, grabbed the shark and reeled it in while Frank swam over my back to help out. We did three or four passes, and finally it got so dark we couldn't shoot any more. Thank God.

We got the shark back in the boat, and Frank said he wanted to freeze it so we could use it as a backup the next day. We took it back to the Santa Monica pier where they had an icehouse. The next day we went out and again didn't have much luck shark hunting. Finally, Frank said, "We'll use the frozen shark."

"OK, well, that's better," I thought to myself.

After a bit, the shark limbered up and looked more like the real deal, so we started to shoot. The shoot took a couple of hours. Frank and the camera-man had wetsuits on, but I didn't; I was still in my sarong, bra, and wig to look like a girl in the water, and I was getting cold. Then Frank wanted me to play the part of the guy, catch the shark, knife it, and kill it – the big shark fight.

I dressed in long pants and a shirt and doubled as the guy. I had been in the water for a while and was getting even colder and more tired. As we were talking over the next shot, the camera guy looked down and yelled, "Shark!" While we had been shooting, the skiff had still been chumming, and now we were surrounded by sharks.

We looked down and saw a big blue shark coming straight at us. It was a big shark, way bigger than me. Frank yelled, "Get this thing outta here!" and he handed me the mako.

They say you can't walk on water, but they're wrong; I walked on water that day. I was scared to death, and I got that 150-pound mako back to the boat pretty fast.

Frank Donahue. *Bev Morgan*

Ronnie Hodge, the "Snowman," on the left, then Mike Stang, Bob Bermel, and me (I was buff at one time). To my right are Les Arndt and then Del Cannon. Hawai'i. *Mickey Muñoz Collection*

Living in Hawai'i

One time when I was in Hawai'i, I was staying next to Jerry's Sweet Shop. Del Cannon and I were roommates and paid about $9 a month. We lived on rice and stolen pineapples and bananas: We were pretty broke. A fellow we knew came and asked us if we could help him get his outrigger sailing canoe in from the anchorage off Hale'iwa. So we swam out, pulled the anchor, and got the boat in to the beach. In reward, he bought us a gallon bottle of wine.

Greg Noll and I sat on the wall in front of Jerry's, drank the wine, and got shit-faced. We attracted the angry attention of four Hawaiians from farther up the North Shore who were also drunk. Greg went off to get help, and the Hawaiians took the opportunity to beat the shit out of me, throw me off the wall to the coral below, and grab the rest of the wine. I staggered back down the street to find Greg with a couple other people in tow. Needless to say, I was a little upset with Greg: the biggest guy on the North Shore leaving the littlest guy on the North Shore to deal with the drunk *mokes.*

Two nights later, Mike Stang and I were walking by a bar and I recognized the Hawaiian's car. Stang was pumped up and told me, "Let's go in there and confront 'em."

So the two littlest guys on the North Shore went into the bar to take on the big Hawaiians. They were drinking and hooting and – in their Hawaiian way – they were badderass than we were. But we stood back-to-back and confronted them, and they were in shock.

They were so impressed that we would do that – that we had the balls to do that – most *haoles* would have run, and we didn't. One of them said, "You guys are one good *haoles,* we take care of you, you drink with us, and anybody messes with you, let us know." We thought, chuckling to ourselves and thinking of Greg, "As a matter of fact we do have somebody we'd like you to take care of."

ABOVE:
Duke Kahanamoku sitting in the back, next to him is Butch Van Artsdalen, with me and Fred Hemmings in front. Makaha.
Mickey Muñoz Collection

LEFT:
Les Arndt standing by the front fender; the "Snowman," Ronnie Hodge, in the middle and me aft. Hawai'i.
Mickey Muñoz Collection

The Wave
Behind
the Wave

One of the fun little things that we used to do, especially around Laguna Beach because of the way the beach is set up, was to ride the wave behind the wave. On very small days with a moderate high tide, the very small waves break right on the beach. Unless you were six inches tall, you weren't going to be able to ride those waves. But behind that wave that broke on the beach, there would sometimes be a little follow-up wave. The wave in front had built up enough water on the beach, and the little wave behind it was actually rideable. So we used to muck around and ride the wave behind the wave, and we got fairly good at it.

A friend in Laguna was the perfect guy to teach riding the wave behind the wave. So one day, he and I went out to ride the wave behind the wave, and we had a blast. It was a beautiful glassy day with no one around, and we got wave after wave. Sometimes this wave behind the wave would turn and go down the beach and you could ride close to a city block down the beach in four or five inches of water. My friend became obsessed with it.

I moved out of Laguna, and years later I was going through the Hobie manufacturing shop. The boards were all lined up in the racks with their order cards. I was with Jim Galoon, and I was thumbing through these boards. I came across a board that looked way different from the rest, and I could see this smile come across Jim's face. I purposely put my hands over the order card and told him, ''I know exactly who this board is for! I know who designed this board, who it's for, and what it's for.''

It was for my Laguna friend, and it was a finless board designed specifically for riding the wave behind the wave. There are no bad waves.

Tom Morey got me all excited about a wave pool where the water was only a few inches deep and they wouldn't allow fins. I dreamed up this finless board to ride that, but I also rode it in ocean waves. *Mickey Muñoz*

I don't know what that says, except that there are a lot of little niches in surfing. There were in the past, and there are in the present. Look at the finless resurgence. In all due respect to the ability of surfers doing airs and other progressive maneuvers, the thruster came into vogue, became the standard, and tuned out everything else. There's so much more to surfing than riding a thruster.

People are revisiting the past with the *alaia* boards, the *olos*, and the other finless boards. People are experimenting with contemporary fish and '70s fish, twin-fins, single-fins, three fins, four fins, five fins, stand-up. Surfing doesn't even have to be on a surfboard. You can surf a 70-foot sailboat downwind in the middle of the ocean. You can surf on a mat, a piece of wood, a hand-plane, you can bodysurf . . . you can mindsurf.

RIGHT: **Salt Creek.** *Sam Olson*
BELOW: **Cabo.** *Jeff Divine*

Carter Pyle and P-Cats

I got my first taste of sailing on Malibu Outriggers. The Malibu crew had 15 or 20 of them on the beach right by the Malibu Pier where they had an outrigger club also on the beach. The boats were just under 20 feet long and were built out of bent plywood – no fancy curves or reverse curves, all home built to a set of plans. They had a single main hull, an outrigger, and a lanteen rig. They turned out to be very efficient boats.

Warren Seaman designed the boat, and his son Roy went on to have a lot to do with designing later catamarans. Joe Quigg and Matt Kivlin were both into sailing and racing them. A lot of the surfers in Malibu were into those outriggers, and they all built their boats.

My next sailing opportunity came along when they sailed *Waikiki Surf* from Hawai'i to the mainland. That was the first catamaran, as far as I know, to be sailed over from Hawai'i. They planned to sail it back in the Transpac, and I was supposed to be on the crew. I had to get a letter from my parents saying I could go because I was so young, but the owner's lawyer finally put his foot down and said it was too much risk. I was on the boat, and we were getting towed out to the starting line – I had already stowed my gear – and they kicked me off just before the start.

It turned out to be a really radical race – a lot of wind and big waves. It scared the shit out of Buzzy Trent who was on the crew and as familiar as anybody with big waves, but they made it, and I wish I had gone.

Much later, after I married Diane, I was in Laguna and got invited to a party. At the party, Flippy Hoffman asked if I remembered Carter Pyle. I had met Carter in Hawai'i in 1954. Carter hung out around Newport. He went to Stanford and was a football player there, then went to Hawai'i and played football for the Navy. Mostly he was there to surf, though. He was a real smart guy and a real water guy. At the party, Flippy told me that Carter was prototyping a catamaran that he wanted to build in production, and he needed help. The day after the party, I went up to Carter's place in Costa Mesa, and he hired me to work in his catamaran-building business.

By then Joe Quigg was also in Newport building boards and was starting the process of building his first large catamaran. All three of us would take our lunch down at the beach and bodysurf the Wedge. Carter and Quigg would commiserate for two or three hours at the Wedge during those lunches and talk catamarans and design. I soaked up their conversation. I was building the boats, demoing them, racing them, cruising them, and helping to sell them. We built some other designs at Newport Boats like the International Finn, a very progressive 15-foot planing dingy unirigged on an unsupported mast, which had the second-highest official sailboat speed record at that time. I ended up working for him for about seven years.

ABOVE:
Tommy Carlin on the helm, me on the bow, with
Bob Andre by the mast of a P-Cat as we get
towed out to the start of the Ensenada Race. We
loved to costume out, so we're wearing plastic
tanker helmets and ski goggles. Newport Beach.
Tom Keck

OPPOSITE PAGE:
Carter and I moving the boat well in the Newport to
Ensenada race. I mostly raced it on catamarans, and
we were usually either first to finish or right up in
front. *Tom Keck*

Bodysurfing
the Wedge

While I was working for Carter, we would go down to the Wedge a lot. But as his business grew, he hired more people, and he couldn't be seen going down to the Wedge every day at lunch with me. So I would leave first and walk down the street out of sight of the shop, he would leave later in his car and pick me up, and off to the Wedge we'd go for lunch. We would meet Joe down there. We would have an hour and a half in the water and half an hour to bolt down lunch, get back, and surreptitiously slide back into the shop individually and with salt caked on us from the ocean. Everybody knew what we were doing.

Here I'm flanked by Buzzy Bent in the foreground and Bobby Patterson behind as we check out the Wedge. Newport Beach. *Bev Morgan*

We rode the Wedge big, we rode it small, we rode it in all its shapes and forms; we rode it every day it was breaking – for years. The Wedge felt like home for me: I was a swimmer to begin with, and I learned to bodysurf before I learned to surf. I've always loved the simplicity of bodysurfing and the idea of shaping the body for the wave.

The second time I went to Hawai'i in '57, when I rode Waimea. I went to Makaha a lot. I probably spent more time bodysurfing Makaha than I did board surfing there. The place had quite a group of bodysurfing locals. They wouldn't even talk to me at first, but eventually one of the older guys, Noah Kalama, was impressed by how much time I spent in the water and that a *haole* was out there bodysurfing. He took me under his wing and taught me how to really bodysurf. Noah was a fabulous waterman and a great bodysurfer.

What I learned there helped me at the Wedge. The Wedge has a whole other set of rules than Makaha. The techniques were similar, but the Wedge can get pretty surly. It can pitch you out feet first, face down, drop you on dry sand, and just pummel you, but it was quite a wave. When you got a really good wave at the Wedge, it was worth talking about. Maybe it would be one wave a go-out. On certain days, you'd get a half a dozen or dozen; other days you wouldn't get any. You might go days without getting any good waves, but when you got one, especially the backdoor ones, you would get a long ride and would be flying so fast it would make it all worth it.

I experimented with fins and started designing and making my own fins for bodysurfing there. The stupidest thing I did was to take a pair of old football shoes and a pair of duck feet; then I added a foot or more onto the duck feet with plywood and then lashed the whole set up onto my football shoes. I was trying to increase the initial underwater thrust – the first one or two kicks that got you into the wave. I almost broke my legs.

The Wedge was all about prepositioning. You had to be in the right spot at the right time to get into the wave and down the face; otherwise, you went over the falls and got killed. Timing was everything. I loved bodysurfing; when I lived in Laguna, I won the Brook Street bodysurfing contest for a number of years in a row.

One of the inventions that I have really fantasized about a lot is a total bodysurfing costume. Why not be the surfboard? Why not be a sea lion or a dolphin? I think it's possible, and it has been really tempting, but you know, there's just not enough time in life to do all these things.

TOP TWO: **Carter Pyle, Phil Edwards and me at the Wedge.** *Bev Morgan*

BOTTOM: **Again, Mickey closest to the curl. Buzzy Trent gets credit for that.** *Bud Browne*

Dora and
the Dark Side

BELOW:
Miki Dora. Sunset. *Don James*

OPPOSITE PAGE:
Miki Dora. Malibu. *Grant Rohloff*

At the north end of Laguna, on the ocean side, there used to be a little family-run restaurant by the name of Van's – a husband and wife team, both in their 60s and both the nicest people you could meet. You'd walk in and order a dinner, and if the dinner included a baked potato, they would wash the potato, put the potato in the oven, and bake the potato. The food was never made ahead of time; it was always made after you ordered it.

When you finished your dinner they would ask, "Did you get enough? Can we bring you more?" If you said yes, they would bring you more food and keep feeding you until you were full. It wasn't just the individual portion you paid for; they fed you till you were full. And the desserts were wonderful.

I had been surfing Trestles with Miki Dora and some other friends, and we were on our way back up north. There were four or five of us surf rats, and we went to have this great lunch at Vans. Dora told us, "Don't worry about the tab, I'm paying for it."

After we were done, Mrs. Van asked in her real squeaky voice, "Boys, we have pumpkin pie, banana cream pie . . ." and on and on. So we ordered this wonderful dessert to top off our lunch.

Then Dora got up and went to the bathroom. We got up and thanked Mrs. Van, went out the door, and got in the car. Then Dora came out with Mrs. Van following behind. She said, "Boys, boys. I don't know what happened here, but you forgot to pay for your lunch." Dora mumbled something, trying to scam his way out of it.

Mrs. Van continued, "You know, I'll tell you what. I know it costs a lot of money; I'd like to buy that lunch for you. And thank you very much for coming in." I felt about an inch tall as we drove away.

I don't know whether it ever affected Dora or not, but that was a lesson I'll never forget; Mrs. Van knew exactly what had happened, and she threw the ball back into our court. She did it in such a way that it made a deep impression on me. I suspect that Dora's take on it was, "If I don't do it, somebody else will, so it might as well be me. If a person is that much of a sucker, then they deserve it."

Dora was a scammer, and I tried out that lifestyle. I once got caught boosting records from a record store, and it was the most embarrassing, horrible thing in my life. They called my parents and the cops. I was humiliated and that was it. Dora went his way; I went my way, and yet, over the years our lives would bring us back together briefly in places in the world. I respected his intelligence, his creativity, and obviously, his surfing prowess. He was interesting, but our ethics were different, and I just couldn't hang out with him as a buddy.

Checking in at the noseriding competition. The official is inspecting Rusty Miller's (squatting in the yellow jacket) and Mike Doyle's boards. They ultimately decided that the wood glassed onto the tails was not in the spirit of the competition. *Bruce Brown*

Morey's Noseriding Competition

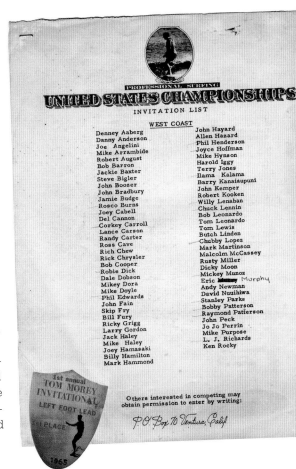

The Tom Morey Invitational was a noseriding competition, held at C Street in Ventura, with a cash prize. Being a pointbreak, C Street was a great place to host it; it had plenty of parking, plenty of waves, and there were places you could practice out of the competition area. The prize was awarded to the longest accumulated time on the front fourth of the board length – there was a line on your board that was 25 percent of the length back from the nose. If both heels were forward of that line, you were considered on the nose of the board.

The way they judged it was pretty interesting. Each judge had two timers with a stopwatch. Those timers had their backs to the waves. The judge would say, "Start, stop, start, stop, start, stop," whenever the rider was forward of the line on a wave. The judges were separated far enough apart that they could see the wave from a slightly different angle and weren't an influence on each other's calls. It was as objective as it could be.

Everybody came up with different noseriding designs for the contest. The Hobie team riders got together to design our own entry. I got together with Phil Edwards, and I had some ideas on concaves, lift, and drag and all of that.

Phil shaped my first board for the competition, and I tried it out. We then conferred, came up with some tweaks, and tried them out; we did some experimenting. We made two or three versions before we concluded that we were on the right track. One board I made was purple with a big gold dollar sign on the nose in front of the line. That was where the money was.

A lot of the other competitors relied on skill or trickery. Some glassed two-by-fours on the tails of their board to lengthen their board. That made the line marking the first 25 percent of board farther back on the surfboard; basically if you included the length of the two-by-four, they were riding their whole board as the nose. At the last minute Tom said no to that, and they had to saw the two-by-fours off. Others glassed a brick on the tail, thinking it would counter their weight on the nose. All that was just trickery, no function at all, and Tom wouldn't let that go.

Noseriding design was all about the rocker and the tail; you want the water to perform the trickery. If you want to lift the nose, then you want the tail to suck down. Water follows curves. Take a spoon and hold it under a water faucet with the cup side up, the water hits that cup and goes off the edge in a spray. But if you turn it so the cup side is down, the water gets sucked around that curve. If you think about it that way, you put a lot of rocker in the tail; the water is going to travel around that curve and suck the tail down.

The contest was pooh-poohed by a lot of people: "It's just noseriding; it has nothing to do with the rest of surfing." That was true to some extent, but what we learned from that far out on the design pendulum swing was what makes a board nose-ride and what happens when you get back on the tail and get on that rocker. Boards previous to this didn't have much rocker in the tail. A lot of what we learned has been passed down into current board design, both shortboards and longboards.

Phil Edwards tests a noseriding board prototype at Lowers.
Mickey Muñoz

PROFESSIONAL SURFING UNITED STATES CHAMPIONSHIPS

INVITATION LIST

WEST COAST

Denney Aaberg	John Hayard
Danny Anderson	Allen Hazard
Joe Angelini	Phil Henderson
Mike Arrambide	Joyce Hoffman
Robert August	Mike Hynson
Bob Barron	Harold Iggy
Jackie Baxter	Terry Jones
Steve Bigler	Ilama Kalama
John Boozer	Barry Kanaiaupuni
John Bradbury	John Kemper
Jamie Budge	Robert Kooken
Rosco Burns	Willy Lenahan
Joey Cabell	Chuck Lennin
Del Cannon	Bob Leonardo
Corkey Carroll	Tom Leonardo
Lance Carson	Tom Lewis
Randy Carter	Butch Linden
Ross Cave	Chubby Lopez
Rich Chew	Mark Martinson
Rick Chrysler	Malcolm McCassey
Bob Cooper	Rusty Miller
Robie Dick	Dicky Moon
Dale Dobson	Mickey Munoz
Mikey Dora	Eric Murphy
Mike Doyle	Andy Newman
Phil Edwards	David Nuuihiwa
John Fain	Stanley Parks
Skip Fry	Bobby Patterson
Bill Fury	Raymond Patterson
Ricky Grigg	John Peck
Larry Gordon	Jo Jo Perrin
Jack Haley	Mike Purpose
Mike Haley	L. J. Richards
Joey Hamasaki	Ken Rocky
Billy Hamilton	
Mark Hammond	

Others interested in competing may obtain permission to enter by writing:

P.O. Box 70 Ventura, Calif.

1st annual TOM MOREY INVITATIONAL LEFT FOOT LEAD 1st PLACE 1965

Bear Wrestling

I was hired by a sports and vacation show. They'd set up a big canvas pool and wanted to know if I could go tandem with a gal on a surfboard while being towed across the pool. I said of course I could. They paid my way to Chicago, and off I went. I was a jack-of-all-trades. I worked with a dog team act. I worked with some tumblers. There was an ex-pro wrestler who had a bear-wrestling act. He needed a shill to come out of the audience and wrestle the bear. The bear was a 400-pound black bear that loved beer and coke and had a tongue on him about a foot long. He actually had some good moves. There is no way you're going to beat a bear. In 20 tries, I managed to get him down once. My strategy was to raise my arms and stand up tall, which he would mimic, then dive down, grab him around the ankles and try to topple him over. The bigger the guy, the easier it was for the bear. He'd been declawed and defanged, but he'd grab these guys and lick them in the face with his big stinky tongue, and the crowd loved it. He had a tough time with me. I was small and could squirm around.

Down for the count: bear wrestling in Chicago.
Mickey Muñoz Collection

Demolition
Days

Before I met Frank Donahue, I got to know a guy named Courtney Brown, who was a stunt double for Lloyd Bridges. Courtney took me to Malibu and introduced me to scuba diving. He put the lung on me and showed me how it was done; he told me the most important thing to remember is you have to breathe on the way up, don't hold your breath. I got under water, took a breath and started to giggle, then the giggle grew into a laugh. It was the most incredible experience of my life; I had been holding my breath going under waves all this time, and now I was able to breathe under water. It was amazing.

The next time I got to dive with a lung, I was in the Bahamas with Tom Carlin. He had a P-Cat he wanted me to bring to him in the Bahamas. He'd moved from California and was working there on movies. He asked me if I would drive his Volkswagen van and tow his P-Cat to the East Coast. It was a long solo drive. Somewhere in Texas I got out and found a stick just the right length to prop between the accelerator and the dashboard so I could sit cross-legged in the seat. By the time I got to Houston, the van needed a valve job, but I knew people in Houston that I could stay with. I eventually got to Florida and dropped off the boat and the car to be shipped over and then flew to the Bahamas. We surfed some outer reefs that had never been surfed, but Tom was also working on an underwater film.

In the Bahamas, if it's not 200-foot visibility, they don't film; that was a pretty different experience than 5- to 10-foot visibility at Malibu. The crew worked off an 85-foot barge with a compressor onboard filling tanks and people sorting out all your gear. With unlimited air, I got to breath underwater for hours every day. The water was 85 degrees – at 100 feet it was the same temperature – and crystal clear. So the second time I ever had an aqualung on I was in the Bahamas in crystal clear water and falling backward – no wetsuit, no buoyancy compensator, no weight, none of that bullshit – just falling backward watching this barge fly away upward. It was like I was suspended and the barge was flying away from me. I got to hang out with these guys for a week while they worked on this film; it was a great experience.

Later on, Tom moved back to California and lived on Coronado Island while traveling all over doing film work and underwater construction. He got hired as part of the crew to demolish the old Capistrano pier; he hired me because I had local knowledge of the area. That job was my introduction to blowing up piers.

My first day on the job I was unloading a pickup truck full of cases of dynamite. Out of the blue the dynamite guy opened one of the boxes of dynamite in the back of his pickup and threw a stick at me. "Oh shit!" I thought.

"Don't worry," he told me, "that's a good fresh piece, no problem. You can throw that stuff around all day, but if you find one that's broken and starting to ooze white crystals, that's the one you want to be careful with. That's nitroglycerin; you don't want to muck with that. Those are the bad ones, but these are the good ones," he laughed.

"Fire in the hole!" Bringing down the pier in Long Beach.
Mickey Muñoz Collection

That was the test, to see if I had the *cojones* to do this. The dynamite guy was highly experienced; he used explosives like the other guys used chainsaws to cut the headers or blowtorches to cut steel. He finally blew his hands off later on some other job.

My contribution to the Capistrano pier job was to introduce the surfboard into the underwater construction business. I don't think anybody had used a board before. It worked great as a shuttle in the surf zone, and there was a lot of surf during that job. We ended up finishing the job 50 percent faster than scheduled partially because of the surfboard.

Our next job was to demo the pier in Long Beach. On that job I got to set the charges, run the trunk line, crimp the fuse, and light it off. I got it all done, shouted "Fire in the hole!" lit the fuse, and paddled back to the boat. I got on the boat. Nothing. A full minute went by. Nothing. Two minutes. Three. Still nothing. Technically, you're supposed to wait hours and then you go in with special fire suits. But in the construction business, there isn't time for that. So the demo expert said, "OK, I've got to go in and disarm the charge."

I replied, "No, I set it. It's my responsibility. I must have screwed up."

He said, "Well . . . OK. Here's what you do . . . "

So I paddle in on my board, over 80 pounds of dynamite, to check the fuse and cut the trunk line below the cap. I was just shaking, very nervous. I got it all set up again and went back to the boat. Two minutes, three, four, five, 10 . . . nothing happened. Shit, I had to go in again! This time we discovered that the fuse was faulty; there were gaps in the powder train. I went back underwater to reset the whole line, reset the cap and fuse. "Fire in the hole!" The last section came down.

We made up what we called "wiener schnitzels." We'd insert eight sticks of dynamite through flexible plastic tubing, two abreast, and then run a length of prima cord through it. We'd make up a bunch of these "sausages" and tie them around our waists, our neck, and our arms – wherever we could fit them – then diving with tanks, we would swim to a piling, work our way down to the base, and tie a "wiener schnitzel" around it. Then we'd grope our way to the next piling and so on till we tied in all our charges. Then we had to backtrack, running the trunk line to connect all the charges. That line would come out of the water and connect to the detonator. The visibility was zero; it was all done by feel. You had to crawl through all the shit that had fallen or been thrown off the pier: tires, bikes, cars, shopping carts, washing machines, steel pipes, rods, tubes, cats, fish, bodies . . . 100 years of it. Not to mention there was a lot surf, so every time a set would come through, you would be violently dragged in one direction then another. It was lovely.

Meanwhile, on the pier was a guy with a chainsaw cutting through all the wood – huge header beams and planking. Another guy with a torch was cutting all the steel – sewer pipes, electrical conduit, water pipes, and gas lines. We were taking the pier out in 60-foot sections. When everything was clear, we'd detonate a charge, which sheared the pilings off at the base, after which we had tons of shit in the water that we had to get into the beach before we went to the next section.

That's where the surfboard came in. Rather than try to get a boat in and out through the surf, I could paddle and surf my way in and out faster. I would haul a tag line out from the beach, connect it to a load – which got pretty hairy at times with breaking waves – then they'd pull it out of the water with a D-9, stack it, and haul it away. It was quite an operation.

The job was going pretty well, and we were about halfway done. I was tying off my last charge and about ready to surface and swim back to the boat to get the trunk line, resubmerge, and connect all the pilings together. Suddenly the piling I was working on started to move. They would move when a set would come through, but there was no set. "I better get out of here." As I swam up and away from the pier the whole 60-foot section collapsed: giant beams, pilings, and steel.

It took about 10 days to drop the whole pier and clear the water of debris, but there were still pilings underwater that were left, and the surf had come up double overhead. We had to clean out what was left of the pilings that had been broken off, and the only way you could do it was to blow them out. It was the most uncomfortable I've ever been in the ocean. We'd anchor the boat and get out and dive down with a line into pitch black, crawling on the bottom. A set would come through and we'd be swept 50 feet, totally out of control. It was a war zone. After about 20 minutes, Carlin and I came up, looked at each other, and agreed we got them all. "I want outta here!" "Me too!"

ABOVE:
I'm the handsome devil leaning against the railing with the yellow hard hat. Capo Beach pier.
Mickey Muñoz Collection

OPPOSITE PAGE:
If I look nervous, it's because I am: I have to go back in and reset 60-pounds of dynamite that has a faulty fuse. Long Beach pier.
Mickey Muñoz Collection

Bob McTavish

I was one of a group of California surfers on a trip around the South Pacific in 1968 for a film project called *The Fantastic Plastic Machine*. The film told the story of the longboard to shortboard transition. Our group was all on longboards when we left California. When we landed in Australia, the first guy I met off the plane was Bob McTavish. We got along like we were long-lost brothers. He was a driving force in contemporary board design, which at that time in Australia was wide-tailed, deep-vee'd, shorter boards. They were much more maneuverable than the boards we were riding. It was the beginning of the era where you had to pump and skate your board to make a wave rather than just aim and fire.

McTavish showed us his latest dream creations: deep concave channels on each side of a center vee – very spacey and really interesting. I was so taken by what they were doing that immediately on my return from that trip I made a series of very deep vee shortboards for California.

I knew they were happening, but the affirmation came for me on a huge day at Rincon when we were taking off near the second point and making it through to the beach. I took off behind Corny Cole. We rode from the second point through the first point, way down to the coast highway: It was a long, fast ride. Corny was an aim-and-fire type rider on a long, heavy board. I was riding one of my short deep vees, making two or three turns to every maneuver he was making.

I probably traveled a third more distance than he did and ended up in the same place at the same time. That verified the smaller, more maneuverable boards for me. Luckily, I was small enough to make the transition fairly easily. Very quickly, these boards evolved to have subtler vees, more tail rocker, narrower tails, concaves, slots, wings, more efficient planing surfaces, and multiple fins to control the speed.

Bob McTavish shows off the groundbreaking bottom contours of his deep vee shape. As soon as I got back to California, I started experimenting with this idea in my boards. Australia.
Mickey Muñoz

Building *Malia*

I was hanging out in Newport with hot-shit sailboat racers. I had worked on some big boats there, learned to varnish, learned to rebuild winches, and do all the boat stuff. I was really getting into boats, and I was saving fittings here and there and stuff that was cast away while building P-Cats with Carter Pyle. I had boxes of this stuff, and I thought to myself, "Hmm, I have enough stuff here to build a boat."

Joe Quigg had finished his boat. Flippy Hoffman bought the mold from Joe, and I helped Flippy build his boat from that mold. I asked Flippy if I could borrow the mold to start my own boat, which I would call *Malia*. I modified the hulls so much that they ended up nothing like the originals; I kept tweaking them. The way I built my boat it would have been a lot easier if I hadn't used the mold. It was a huge learning process for me in engineering and design. It was a massive project.

The inspiration came from Joe and Carter of course, but also from Phil Edwards building *El Gato* and seeing that boat develop. Phil used different materials: He built his boat out of plywood and glass; I built out of foam and glass. Phil's had a solid wing where mine basically had two tubes that held the boat together and supported the trampoline. *Malia*'s hulls were symmetrical displacement hulls. I put a subdeck inside the hulls and then built a fairing on each hull that looked like the windshield on an airplane, with a little cockpit behind it with a seating area. I put in a cabin door underneath the fairing that protected the inside of the hull; there was enough room inside that you could sleep there.

I was married to Diane at the time, and we were living in Dana Point in a little Spanish house. I had to make an extendo on the single-car garage to be able to do the mold work and lay up the hulls. I had designed the boat to be modular so that I could finish each piece independently without actually putting them all together. That solved the issue of not having enough space to build the whole thing in one piece. After Diane and I got divorced, I moved the boat and myself to the "Alley of Broken Dreams." That was what we called the alley behind Hobie's shop where all the failed or obsolete projects ended up. I had a shaping room in the adjoining shop and lived in the alley in my van for the next year, working and finishing the boat.

We launched her at Poche. Flippy's boat was the midwife, and we pulled her out of the womb and through the surf, then sailed her up to the harbor. I paid a guest slip fee for the night; the next day I sailed her to Newport Beach, and the next morning sailed her in the Ensenada race. After the race, we cruised back up the coast. We spent two or three days on Todos Santos, surfing and diving there, then sailed back to Coronado Island, slipped through the border and back up to Dana Point.

I didn't have a place to keep *Malia*. I had been on the waiting list at the harbor for three years before the boat was finished, and it took me another three years before I got a slip. In the meantime, I anchored out and paid for a guest slip when I could afford it. *Malia* was homeless.

Then one day I took Pete Siracusa out on her. There was a really good Santa Ana blowing, and I had the boat up in Newport at the time. Pete Siracusa was involved in the second Chart House. In a few years, Pete had made enough money to start the Ancient Mariner/Rusty Pelican chain. Pete was up-and-coming financially and was an avid big boat sailor. I took Pete on my boat in this strong Santa Ana and we sailed to Dana Point. It was the fastest he had ever gone on a boat; we made over 20 knots average from Newport to Dana. When Pete got off the boat he opened his checkbook, wrote a check out to me and signed it but left the date and amount blank. He said, "Whatever you want for the boat, and whenever you want to sell it, just fill in the numbers and the date. I want your boat."

He told me in the meantime if I needed a place to keep her, he would love to have her in front of the Rusty Pelican in Newport; I could have a free slip. I gratefully accepted his offer and told him that he could use the boat any time he wanted. So for three years, I had the boat in front of the Rusty Pelican and sailed it out of Newport. Then my slip came up, and I finally brought her back down to Dana Point.

Malia took seven years just to build and launch: She has taken up most of my adult life as I modified and used her. The boat started out as a pretty fast boat: basically, two hulls, two connecting tubes supporting a trampoline, and a big rotating mast with a fully battened sail. I raced her a little bit, but racing takes total dedication and a lot of money. You've got to constantly modify and upgrade

Flippy Hoffman (l) and Hobie Alter (r) inspect the first of *Malia's* hulls out of Joe Quigg's mold. I had to build the *extendo* on the garage to house the mold. Dana Point. *Mickey Muñoz*

Phil,
Don't laugh, this is jus
some of the thoughts &
I collan de size and weigh
one crossbar on the trailer

To me, the most

So, I sketched a
with the modernizing present day
I would like to do

ROACH IN TOP 3 BATTNS ONLY
SO THAT THE REST OF THE SAIL HAS LESS LOAD
CAN HAVE LIGHTER BATTENS
NO BOOM
AND LIGHTER SAIL CLOTH — EASIER
NO WINDER TO RAISE IT   CHEAPER
                          LIGHTER

RELY ON THE JIBS FOR POWER

ON PERMANENT, INSTANT, SAFE ROLLERS
LESS HASSLE.

I collan de centre board are
8' long and 2' wide
I want something
half that size

stiff I can pick up
by myself.

But,
I not long enough sli
to beat the keel losto

This 40 ft er I'm building for mys
is bigger I land   I am able to
I just don't have   the ability
what I set out to   do. — th
   I'm not able   to make t
that are going on   I'm hang g
wind-surfing etc   I think
I one faster   sooner
maybe 28' or even   a short a

Dana Point, play toy
MOULDED GLASS
PHILL EDWARDS SIZE
27' CATAMARAN
15' WIDE
700 POUND

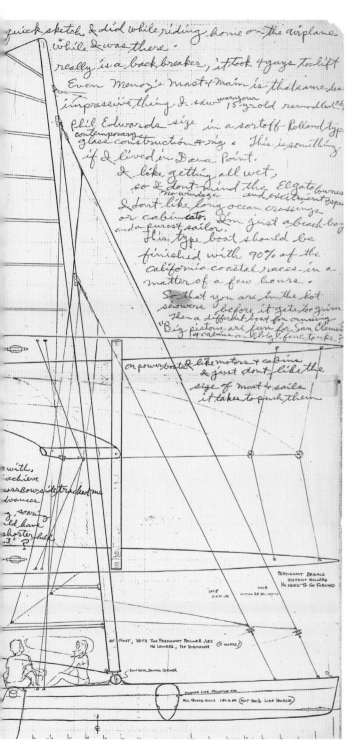

if you want to stay competitive. Unless you have the money to pay for the labor and parts, you have to do it yourself – that cut into my surfing and family time.

The original design was competitive enough. I raced her in the Ensenada race four times. As I grew older and more interested in the cruising side, I kept modifying *Malia* to be more of a cruising boat. I like the efficiency and the speed of a catamaran, as well as the advantages of stable platform at anchor; it's a place to live reasonably comfortably and go diving, fishing, surfing, and exploring.

As *Malia* evolved, I kept putting bigger motors on her. She had a lot of sail area; the mast alone was big enough to capsize her in a big blow. In Southern California, because it is mostly light air, you aim either for very efficient sailing or you go with power. For efficient sailing on a small catamaran you have to go light, which sacrifices load carrying – you end up leaving a lot of beer and toys on the dock. With just power you have to carry a lot of fuel and you are dependent on the engines, but you can generally travel consistently faster than sailing. I tried for a compromise on *Malia*. The best of both worlds: motor sailing on an efficient platform.

Malia was never intended to be an open-ocean boat, but I always visualized sailing her to Hawai'i. I wish I had, but I never did. She ended up in Hawai'i anyway. I designed her so she would come apart and be able to go into a 40-foot container and be shipped anywhere in the world. I figured if I couldn't sail her somewhere, I could take her apart, ship her there, put her back together, and sail her. When I finally sold her to Pua Rochlen, we put her in a container and shipped her to Hawai'i. I took the whole boat apart in three days. It was much more complicated than when I put her together: hundreds of screws and bolts that had been welded by corrosion and time held the boat together. She came apart just like she was designed to do.

I pulled out of that deal with Pua three times in tears. Each time I called Pua in Hawai'i. "I can't do it," I would sob into the phone. Peggy was in tears too; we had our first and second date on *Malia*. She loved her.

It was really hard to sell *Malia*. Most of my adult life had been tied up in building and modifying that boat. But she was never going to be anything more than a camping platform – a highly efficient camping platform – but a camping platform nonetheless. I had taken her as far as I could. As I grew older, I wanted something more comfortable and easier to sail. So I ended up selling her.

LEFT:
A sketch by Joe Quigg addressed to Phil Edwards and passed on to me while I was building *Malia*.

OPPOSITE PAGE CLOCKWISE FROM TOP LEFT:
Malia on the backside of Catalina Island. *Mickey Muñoz*

Nearing completion, one of *Malia*'s hulls rests in Hobie's "Alley of Broken Dreams." *Mickey Muñoz*

Malia at speed; she was a fast boat in her day. *Geri Conser*

The chaos of cruising mode: sleeping on *Malia* was basically a camping setup. *Mickey Muñoz*

A lot of my friends came down to help me put her in the water the first time: On the left in the cap and red shirt is Brennan "Hevs" McClelland, to the right of him with his ever-present cigarette is Ronald Patterson, in the red shirt with the full beard is Bud Platten who was also a boat builder, and that's my son Miguel in the yellow tee shirt. Poche. *Mickey Muñoz Collection*

Malia on the beach at Poche for her regular maintenance and modification. *Mikey Muñoz*

A Different Way to Build Boats

Hobie's genius in designing the Hobie Cat was that he adapted the surfboard-building process to the boat-building world. When building a surfboard, the buyer comes in and orders a custom board. He or she talks it over with the shaper; the shaper builds the board, glasses it, and out it goes. The customer rides it, gives feedback, and the next time around you get a better board. In boat building, you don't get too much of that; the commitment, expense, and length of time is so much greater that you usually only get one shot at it. Hobie, because of his experience in surfboard building, designed a different system for building boats.

First he considered what sort of boat made sense to build. Hobie was interested in surfing; he wanted to go fast; he wanted a boat he could launch through the surf and ride a wave into the beach. He didn't want to worry about sticking dagger boards or rudders into the sand. Catamarans made sense to him. They were agile and quick; you could ride waves with them in the middle of the ocean or on the beach. He wanted the rudders to kick up, and the hulls to have enough lateral resistance that the boat could go to weather without dagger boards. These were the priorities he came up with before even designing the boat.

Then Hobie invented this universal platform to attach the hulls to that was light and served to hold the mast and the rigging. Hobie set to work prototyping different hulls shaped from foam and glass that were built just like a surfboard. Hobie would shape the hull for one side and he would have one of the other shapers, including me, shape the hull for the other side and then we would go for a sail and see how the boat sailed on the different tacks. We were knocking them out like surfboards. We could shape a hull in a day, glass it, and have it in the water two days later.

We tested many different hulls. We would take pictures and see how the boat sailed on the different hulls, and we started zeroing it in. I don't know how many prototypes we made, but I know we made dozens just in developing that one boat. Most boat designers only get a few dozen in their lifetime.

It's because we were shapers that we got into all that design R&D. We shaped foam and balsa, and we got into carbon and other exotic composites. It was natural for us to get into airfoils and airplanes: We were already shaping foils for the water in the manner of boards, fins, and rudders. We had all that good lift off the bluff at Dana Point, and the land above was empty. We would hand launch gliders off of there, and then Hobie got into radio control. Hobie designed his radio-controlled model glider, the Hobie Hawk, that he put into production. It's still a classic, just a beautiful airplane.

ABOVE: Phil Edwards, in aviator cap and goggles, gets ready to launch one of his designs off the Dana Point bluff. We got into model airplanes for a while and would make them from scrap balsa left over from building boards. *Mickey Muñoz*

OPPOSITE PAGE: In this Hobie ad shot, Hobie and I are wearing one of the first wetsuits made specifically for surfing that we helped Bev Morgan design. That was the beginning of Body Glove. *Mickey Muñoz Collection*

A Small Boat
in a Big Race

The first time that Carter Pyle and I raced a P-Cat to Ensenada, we used a road map as a chart. I think we were the second boat to finish overall, despite blowing it and overstanding the mark. We didn't know where we were going or what the course exactly was; we just sailed the boat.

My most memorable adventures in the Ensenada race on small cats happened on a boat we called the *Super 16*. We took a Hobie 16 production catamaran, widened it to 10 feet, built in dagger boards so it went to weather better, and put a 32-foot mast on it with a big 180-foot, roller-furling, reaching sail. That was a tall rig and a lot of sail area for that size boat, and it went fast. Out of four races on that boat to Ensenada, we only made it twice. I don't remember the details of the races we finished, but I do remember the times we didn't make it.

The first time we didn't make it, I was racing with Hobie. We were building boards, building boats, and doing other things. Then the Ensenada race would come along, and we had to get our act together. It was a lot of work to do that race. You had to go over every detail to prep the boat and the logistics. We had to get a guy to drive my van down to Ensenada so we could load the boat on it and drive it back up.

I worked most of the night before the race, got up early, launched the boat in Newport, and we were on the starting line by 11:00 am for a noon start. The wind only came up to a light south breeze, typical for the Ensenada race. It's supposed to be a downwind race, but a lot of the times it's a south wind that time of year.

By the next morning, we had just cleared Point Loma; we were having a really slow race. Unfortunately, Hobie has this big business deal. He had to fly up to Washington and meet some people; it had been on the schedule long before the race. Hobie had to bail, but I put so much time into prepping for this that I decided to go on alone. So I dropped Hobie off at Coronado; he made a call, got a taxi, and was gone.

I set off to sea again, and by then had been on the boat sailing for some 28 hours, without much sleep the night before. It was about 2:00 in the afternoon, blowing 12, maybe 14, a beauti-

ful day, the sun was out, and I was eating my lunch with my gear laid out on the tramp. All of a sudden a gust of wind came out of nowhere, and I was doing this chimpanzee act trying to sheet out the reacher, get the main out, and counter the heeling motion. Long story short, I ended up capsizing.

The boat turned all the way upside down, and I couldn't right it by myself. All I could realistically do was unhook the mast and get the rigging and sails off and bundled on top of the upside down boat.

I found a red cushion and hooked it to the end of the whisker pole – a pole we used when sailing to trim the reaching sail. Despite the slowness of the race for us, it was even slower for the rest of the racers, so they were catching up and passing me. I waved that red cushion on the end of the pole at every monohull that passed me – some as close as 100 yards. They couldn't have missed me. I had 20 boats go by, and not one of them stopped, not one of them called the Coast Guard, not one of them acknowledged that I was there. There were also a few powerboats coming back from fishing off of Ensenada that I tried to flag down. Those who saw me would detour to avoid me.

I started to think that if these bastards aren't going to stop and help me, I'm going to have to swim for it, so I lashed everything together that would float to aid me. My plan was to give myself the four hours of daylight left to swim to the beach. I figured I was about two and a half or three miles out and it would take me that whole time what with the currents and wind to get into the beach. I wanted enough time to make it before dark.

Just as I was getting ready to swim, I saw a little powerboat coming up right on line with me. To my amazement they didn't avoid me. Onboard were two guys who said they would help me. They called the Coast Guard, and within five minutes the Coast Guard helicopter was there.

I wanted to save my boat, so I waved off the helicopter and talked the guys in the powerboat into helping me right my catamaran. They had to make it back to San Diego in time to clear customs before it closed; otherwise, they would be on their boat all night. I knew the drill on how to right the boat, but it wasn't easy, and after several tries, we weren't able to get it over. They said that we would have to leave it, but I pleaded for

The *Super 16 X1* on the beach at Poche. *Mickey Muñoz*

one more try, and on the last attempt we righted the cat. By then we were in a hurry, and I didn't have time to tie everything on properly. I only had time to get the mast and boom together with the sail wrapped around both and tied together, but not tied to the boat. I ended up lying prone on the trampoline, holding the mast and boom with my hands, and steering with my feet, and we were off. They needed to get back to San Diego.

They were towing me at about 10 knots into the wind and into the bump. The catamaran would ride their wake, catch up, and pass them to the side, then the rope would pull me the other way, and I would cross their wake and catch up to them on the other side. I worked my ass off to avoid hitting them. The cat was bouncing up and down while I was holding on to a couple hundred pounds of gear. I literally held on till blood came out from my fingernail beds. The guys would stop and plead with me to get on the boat and leave all my shit behind, but I couldn't. I had to save it all, and we were almost there; I was confident that we would make it. Finally, we turned the corner into San Diego Bay and tucked into the shelter of Point Loma. They dropped me off at the Coast Guard dock, said their good-byes, and went to clear customs.

In the meantime, a friend who had quit the race because of the light air saw the wreckage and immediately knew that only I could be involved with this mess. He came over and took care of everything. He towed me over to

A small boat in a big race. *Geri Conser*

the San Diego Yacht Club, and everybody came out and carried the boat up into the parking lot and secured a place for it. Then he offered me his boat – which was going to be empty– as a place to stay for the night.

I only had a couple of dollars, but I walked over to the Chart House where they knew me – I was the opening bartender for the Newport Chart House. They took care of me – gave me a free meal with a couple of cocktails.

Next morning, I got up and set out for Ensenada to retrieve my van. I walked to the freeway onramp and stuck out my thumb. The first car that came by was an old American car driven by this big Mexican guy with tats all over him. He looked pretty gnarly. He was only going as far as Tijuana, but that was a start. While we were driving, he told me about all the prisons he had been in and that he was going down to run some drugs back from Tijuana. On hearing that, I started to try to wipe my fingerprints off anything in the car that I had touched.

He asked if I had any money and I replied, "Yeah, I got a couple dollars." He said, "Buy me a beer." So we went to a liquor store and sat drinking beer in some alley in Tijuana while he waited for his contacts.

After the beer, I told him I had to get out of there, and I walked down two blocks and got to Revolución, thinking I would get a ride there easy. I stuck out my thumb and the second car that passed was a Volkswagen bug with three young girls in it. They stopped and asked me where I was going. "Ensenada," I replied, and they said, "Great, we're going there, too." I said, "OK, you want to have fun?" So we stopped at all the right watering holes, and ate and drank our way to Ensenada. We finally got to the Bahia, where the race finished, and they let me off.

It turns out that the racers had held a wake for me because Hobie had reported me missing. After hanging out for a while and enjoying Ensenada, I found my van, drove back to the Yacht Club, and loaded up the boat and came home.

After that capsize fiasco, a friend turned me on to some dry suits. This was before the modern dry suits; they were really just a knockoff of old hard-hat, rubber diving suits. They were a yellow rubber and had a front entry with a rubber band closure; you gathered a bunch of rubber together and tied it off with a band as thick as an inner tube. Wetsuits are wonderful in the water, but they really suck out of the water. The foul weather gear at the time was not very good: It was waterproof, but a sweatbox, and they were clumsy to move around in. I thought that maybe these dry suits would be the answer.

Hobie and I were supposed to do the next Newport to Ensenada race, but at the last minute Hobie couldn't, so I recruited another friend, Dick Petit, who was a sailor, waterman, restaurant owner, and a really good guy.

The *Super 16* on top of one of my old vans at Poche. *Mickey Muñoz*

It was the same drill to get ready: get the van down to Ensenada, prep the boat, and get it to Newport. The next day when the race started, there was a strong south wind, and it looked gnarly. We sailed all day into this wind; it got so bad that Dick got seasick, and seasickness on a small boat is not fun. I was doing most of the work, steering and working the sails. Did I mention there was a lot of sail area for that little boat? About 10:00 or 11:00 that night, conditions got even worse; the south wind was now gusting to over 25 knots.

We had a better angle toward Ensenada on the tack going out than in, so to save my energy, I thought I would go way outside instead of trying to tack back and forth on the inside. I didn't want to get caught in the kelp beds or get too close to the Coronado Islands in the dark. About 10:00 that night, I headed out, and we sailed the whole night out to sea. The next morning we were probably 25 or 30 miles out – pretty far out in a 16-foot catamaran.

Dick was really weak by then. He was too sick to sleep – he hadn't eaten, taken a shit, or peed – he was in a bad way. I hadn't slept because I was steering and working the boat. Finally he said, "You gotta get me to the beach; you gotta get me to the beach now. I'm gonna die." We sailed close-hauled back inshore and came in just below the Coronado Islands.

One of the boats that we were next to on the inside clocked one wind gust at over 55 knots on their wind meter. By then, I had taken down the jib and reefed the main; we were down to a bare minimum of sail area, but we were still making headway and getting there. In a book published later, Skip Dashew, a sailing friend who went on to write some of the foremost books on cruising, included the incident in a chapter on heavy-weather sailing. We didn't qualify as a cruising boat, but a 16-foot boat in a 50-knot wind is pretty heavy-weather sailing.

By the time we got to La Misión, Dick was getting very nervous. La Misión was the last sand beach that we knew of before we got to Ensenada. Dick insisted we go in. We were about a half a mile off the beach, and the waves were breaking all around us and the wind was so strong it was blowing kelp out of the water, and sand filled the air on the beach. We pulled up the daggerboards, got the rudders so they would kick up and tied everything down on the tramp. Then we turned and rode the head-high waves to the beach. Struggling to keep the bows from digging in, we sailed the boat up the 100-yard wide beach. One of the homeowners on the beach gave us showers and dry clothes and then drove us to Ensenada so we could hook up with our people.

Motorcycle
Racing

We got into racing motorcycles, and I loved it. I was in District 37 with the Hobie crew. I raced everything from flat track to desert, scrambles to motocross. I even had a sponsorship on speedway bike – you race on an oval cinder track, with light and powerful bikes with skinny tires and two gears; you're elbow to elbow sliding sideways round the corners at 60 miles an hour. I trained and practiced but never really got to race. It was race or surf!

I ran my Bultaco in an expert practice at Ascot. I went through the half-mile turn as fast as my bike would go – I had it geared for about 90 miles an hour. It was in the morning before the track got dry; the traction was perfect. We were stacked in the corner inches apart, four of us side by side, crossed up and sliding. Everybody was depending on everyone else to keep it together; it was sensual.

We had a little Spanish style house up in Dana Point. I could ride right out of my garage, and within a block and a half from where I lived, I could be in the equivalent of a 20-foot wave; it was all in the right hand. We had hundreds of acres of dirt, all kinds of terrain; we had a dirt-riding paradise.

I started off on a Honda 50, then got a Honda 250. I stripped that bike completely and made all fiberglass parts for it to lighten it up. Then I got sponsored, so I hopped it up. I bored it, polished the ports, special cams, special manifold and exhaust, everything I could do to make it faster. I had different sets of tires to race it on tracks or in the desert. Its demise came when it sucked a valve, driving it through a piston, ruining the cylinder and wiping out the lower end; that ended my Honda sponsorship cause I wasn't that good.

Then I got a 250 Bultaco Pursang. Those bikes were the fastest, lightest, highest horsepower at the time but very sensitive. I put 13 pistons in that bike; the engine seized all the time. I was known as the fastest novice in the world for the first 10 feet, I either "got-off" or the bike would blowup. Next I got sponsored on a Husqvarna and then a Yamaha.

I rode just about everything in the dirt, but my favorite was the desert. It's like the ocean; the sand and dirt form patterns like water does, sand dunes are just slow-moving waves. Riding the desert is like surfing and sailing.

They eventually fenced off the dirt behind Dana Point so they could develop it. The developers hired a caretaker who patrolled it on a Honda 50 with no helmet. We used to get around the fences and do wheelies by him, smiling. He would try to chase us, but he had no chance at all to catch us.

One day, a couple of us turned around after passing him, went back, and said, "Hey, you gotta get a helmet; you gotta get a real bike, you know. You can't be out here on that, you're going to get hurt."

He was so grateful, he told us to keep the noise down, stay out of sight, and he would turn his head. He let us go for a couple more years, but then they finally clamped down and really restricted it.

Meanwhile I hurt my knee on the Bultaco at the first stadium motocross track at Ascot; I was out for over a year with it. It happened when I caught my boot on the footpeg of a bike I was passing. I twisted my foot around and went off a jump like that. It was a flat, hard landing, and the bikes didn't have the suspension they have now. I landed, and my knee just exploded. I finished on one leg and managed to actually qualify.

But I could just feel my knee swelling inside my leathers. I pushed my bike into the back of the truck and left at half time. I knew I couldn't race anymore that day. I went home and had my doctor friend in Laguna look at it. He told me that I had to get it operated on, but I didn't want to do that. Two weeks later, the swelling had gone down, and I could actually run on it. The first wave I took off on, it just went *snap* and *boom*; I was down. I figured if I couldn't surf, I had to get it operated on.

I raced after that a year or so later, but not as much. I came to the realization that I had kids, I wanted to surf, and motorcycle racing was expensive. Maybe I could turn professional, but the younger people were going to beat me; there were just too many of them, and they didn't know they could get hurt. I hung it up after that and got rid of my race bikes. I still cruised around, but I was done with serious racing.

The land behind Dana Point used to be wide open, a dirt biker's paradise. We could ride to Grubby's shop on Crown Valley without crossing a road. Can't do that now. *Mickey Muñoz Collection*

Hang Gliding

I tried hang gliding and skydiving a few times. I learned a lot about the relativity of time while skydiving. I did it on a static line, an umbilical cord basically. You step out of the airplane, and the cord pulls the chute out. You had about three seconds of freefall before the line starts to drag your chute out.

Three seconds doesn't seem like very long, but when you're climbing out the door of an airplane with your feet on the wheel strut and your hand on the wing strut and you're looking down 4,000 or 5,000 feet to the ground below on your first jump, it seems like forever. It's surreal; you're in a pretty heightened state of anxiety and awareness. Time is relative to how fast your brain is operating. It's like being in an auto accident; you can do a hell of a lot of thinking and calculating in the second or two before it happens.

I loved that aspect of skydiving, but it was expensive, and between surfing and building boats, I didn't keep pursuing it. Later on, I decided I'd try hang gliding: I loved the idea of being able to fly.

I took hang gliding lessons, and after ground school instruction covered the basics, they set you up at the top of this hill and you ran downhill until you were airborne, and then you were free – you were flying. On my first flight I overcontrolled a bit but then started to get it. The second flight I went farther and did better. I was starting to understand the dynamics of it and learning where the limits were. The third and fourth flight were better yet. By the fifth flight, I figured I had it down, no problem.

On the last flight of the day, my sixth flight, I really wanted to get a long one. So I asked the instructor if I could go up on the hill as far as I could, launch up there and make some turns. If I could clear the parking lot and go down the next hill, I would get a really long flight. He agreed, so I backed up the hill with my kite and launched.

I can fly! Oops, no I can't! *Crash:* My hang-gliding career was cut short by a VW Bug. *Mickey Muñoz Collection*

I gained altitude: 50 feet, then 75 feet, got into a little left turn, and then angled back the other way in a right turn.

My vision was fixed on the parking lot that I wanted to clear, and I didn't see the Volkswagen coming down the dirt road below me. The driver was going to pick up her boyfriend who had flown off another hill. I was concentrating on getting as much speed and lift as possible to clear the parking lot. I was less than 15 feet off the ground with another 100 feet to go. I knew I could make it, but only by a couple of feet: I was in full trim and calculating how fast I was dropping.

Then I saw her. We were both going about 15 miles per hour and it looked like we were headed for a collision. I did a lot of quick thinking in those several seconds and realized that I wasn't going to make it. I held my line, thinking that the only chance I had was to push the control bar straight forward at the last minute and put the kite in a stall right before we hit and try and pop over the VW. It was the right thing to do – there was no turning, there was no stopping, there was no going up, other than stalling – and it almost worked.

She still hadn't seen me when all of a sudden my right foot came shattering through her closed passenger window. The top of the kite went over the car, but my body didn't. My left foot hit the doorpost, slid off of it, crushing the side of the car, and almost turning it over. I broke the main strut of the kite, and completely wrecked the Volkswagen. The woman driving was in shock; she had no idea what had just happened. People were screaming and running around; my girlfriend at the time thought I had been killed. The instructor, of course, was nearly shitting himself and hoping he had insurance.

I sprained my wrists from pushing on the control bar during the collision, but that was the extent of my injuries. I walked away otherwise unscathed. Then the discussion of who was responsible started, and we both concluded that the person in the air has right of way. That was the end of my hang gliding career.

Getting to the Surf

Vehicles – boats, trucks, vans, cars, bicycles, and skateboards – are a means to an end, just like a surfboard is a means to an end – a way to ride waves.

My vehicles that got me to the surf were like one of Michael Logan's paintings. The underpainting is what makes up the image. Every time I changed, I would change the vehicle, and consequently, each time the vehicle changed, it changed my perspective. I changed the vehicle to either stay up with my perspective or get ahead of it, and I would have to catch up with it. It's kind of like the way surfboard designs have gone. The surfers push the designs and the designs push the surfers.

I'm not a hotel person, and I love to camp. But raising kids, working, being interested in multiple endeavors, and time constraints didn't allow much leisurely kind of camping, so I was more of a car camper – able to move from place to place faster, quicker, easier. I designed my vans with that in mind, and they had to function for both work and play. My vehicles had to be able to get blanks and boards back and forth. I did a lot of boat repairs and boat work. They were constantly full of resin, fiberglass, hand tools, and power tools.

 A van was a good configuration for that because I didn't have to unload all the work stuff and then load all the play stuff: I wanted it all with me all the time.

I started off with the great American automobile design: a Cadillac. The very first thing I did when I got that car was to rip out the back seat and hacksaw and hammer out the cross braces that supported it. I bent, ground, and cut the metal until I made the opening as big as I could. Then I got a used mattress and threw it in there, and that was my bed, and I could lock a board inside. That was my first van, and it has been evolving every since.

If I had held on to my first three or four cars, I could be retired now. Probably one of my best cars was a 1940 Buick limited-edition limousine. It had a spare tire each side of the hood in the front fender wells, a bar in the back, jump seats, and a chauffeur's cabin. It had been a movie car and was well taken care of. I bought it from a dubious character for $200. God, I had a lot of fun in that car.

I've only had one car in my whole life that I bought brand new, and that was a 1969 Econoline Ford van. I put 260,000 miles on it, put a rebuilt engine in it, drove it another 25,000 or 30,000 miles, and sold it to a friend of mine who used it as a work truck. He sold it to a Mexican who filled it with washing machines and TV sets and drove it to Puerto Vallarta. He sold all the stuff he took down there in it, and then he sold the van to a lumberyard. My friend who had bought it as a work truck ended up moving down there 20 or 30 years ago, and he says that my truck is still at work at the lumberyard. God knows how many miles it has on it.

After that, I bought a 1969 E300 bubble-top van, which had standing headroom. It made such a difference. It was horrible for gas mileage, but what a great car. It had positraction and was pretty balanced, so it was good in the dirt, sand, or snow. You could drive that van just about anywhere if you were careful and knew what you were doing. I built a platform rack over the top of the bubble. I could carry boards, boats, and materials on it.

CLOCKWISE FROM TOP LEFT:
Everything in its place. *Mickey Muñoz*

What can I say? I'm a collector. *Mickey Muñoz*

And a place for everything. *Mickey Muñoz*

One of my vans BSC: Before Seat Covers. *Mickey Muñoz*

"Brother" Tompkins, son of "Keyhole" Tompkins, has all he needs for a day, a night, or a lifetime at the beach. *Mickey Muñoz*

Flippy Hoffman

Flippy Hoffman and I met in the mid-1950s; he taught me a lot about the ocean over the course of our time together. Out of the water, he was like an elephant seal; in the water he was all grace.

Flippy was a commercial abalone diver in the 1950s and had been into powerboats his whole life. He wasn't much of a sailor, but I think he respected it. When Phil and I went off into sailboat design and building, Flippy kept ragging on us. "You're doing the wrong thing!" You know, it probably turned out he was right, but it was a great experience.

The evolution of Flippy's boats began with the P-Cat, the catamaran that I helped Carter Pyle build. Flippy bought one and put a little outboard motor on it. That was his first catamaran. From that evolved the *PB&J's 1* and *2* that came out of Joe Quigg's mold. Flippy named those boats after one of his favorite onboard meals.

As a diver and surfer, Flippy wanted simplicity. He didn't want all the bullshit that's on regular boats. He wanted it basically maintenance free. Let the ocean break over it, hit it with a hose afterward, and you're done.

Flippy was always on the leading edge. He wanted to ride all the outside breaks on the North Shore. He had been exploring Ka'ena Point with friends by boat and had ridden there – not 50-footers – but they were paddling into some pretty big ones. So Flippy wanted a "big" board for the outside breaks.

Typical of Flippy, who could have bought Clark Foam, he scrounged a couple of old shitty 12-foot blanks from Grubby, cut the tails off, and then glued the blanks together. It looked like an hourglass. It was 20 feet long when I got it, with a wide redwood stringer down the center. I almost had to have help to turn it over. Jeff Johnson let us use his backyard at 'Ehukai. I outlined the board and shaped it under the trees. First, I had glaring sun, and then the palm branches mottling the light.

It was a great North Shore project with all the kibitzers coming around and lots of *pakalolo* and lots of commenting on design. It wasn't easy under those conditions. Classic Flippy, he had me laminate one of his business cards under the glass with "$5 reward for the return for this board, $10 if it is not dinged" written on it. Of course, it was worth a bit more than that.

It came out at about 70 pounds; it was a big heavy board. I only rode it once. I paddled out at Pūpūkea on a pretty good-sized day. It must have taken me 45 minutes to get out. After I finally got out, I caught one wave and rode it from Pūpūkea to where you paddle out to Pipeline – a long ride. That was it for me; I was done with it.

I think Flippy rode a couple outside reef days, but he really wanted to ride Ka'ena on a big day. Flippy had a funny-looking little skiff with a board rack on it, so we loaded up the boards one day and went out there to see if we could find surf. We never found anything that we could ride.

I later built a more refined version back in my shaping bay on the mainland. We called it the *Awooooooooo* board – what you might yell when you dropped down the face of a big one on it.

Flippy was a brilliant and shrewd business tactician. He could cut straight to the heart of the matter and was able to make business decisions that turned into success. His family was in the fabric business; his dad, Rube, started it in Los Angeles. Neither he nor his brother wanted to inherit the business, but Rube grabbed them by their ears and made them. Flippy wanted to dive for abalone commercially, and his brother, Walter, was in the Navy, and they were both surfers.

ABOVE: This shot gives a good idea of the size of that board. *Mickey Muñoz Collection*

OPPOSITE PAGE: Flippy's 16-foot board for the outer reefs takes shape in Jeff Johnson's North Shore backyard. *Mickey Muñoz Collection*

Surging:
For Every Current
There Is a Countercurrent

In the early years, I had a surf school called the West Coast Surf School. It was probably one of the first ones. One of the basic things I tried to get across to new students was that the power of the ocean was a lot larger than you. Nobody is strong enough to fight it; you have to learn how to flow with it.

I would introduce them to the water by having them lie in the sand. I had them fanned out looking at the water while I was talking about it, talking about the currents and about the ocean's power – where it was, where it went, and how it dissipated. Then I'd tell them, "Just follow me to the water, and we'll go play."

We would breast-stroke down through the sand – like seals – into the very shallowest, 4 to 6 inches of water. From that perspective, a 1-foot wave looked really big. We would just let ourselves go – rolling and tumbling in the power. We would let the power wash us up on the beach and then pull us back out, back in and back out.

Pretty soon they got the feel for the rhythm, for the power and where it took them. We were underwater tumbling. We were facing waves that were bigger than we were because we were only head high. It was really fun. In the process, fear and apprehension were replaced with understanding and respect. We would spend a half hour just playing that way.

Later on when we were doing trips out to the Channel Islands and exploring them by boat, we came up with a game inspired by that experience teaching surfing. We called the game "surging." We would get into an inflatable dinghy and bounce around in the rock gardens and coves. That game taught me a lot.

Our boat had this old Avon inflatable that was 30 or 40 years old at the time. It had a single skin bottom that undulated with the water. It was black and thus warm, and when there was a little bit of wind you could hunch down in it and be in this womblike place, floating on the water. You were dry, warmed by the black tubes, and sheltered from the wind.

The rules of the game were there were no rules, only suggestions. You would take off your watch and leave it on the boat. It was OK to take your sunglasses and hat with you and stuff to keep warm. It was OK to direct yourself by rowing a little bit, but the idea was to row into the rock gardens and coves and let yourself go – to submit completely and let yourself become part of the ocean. You couldn't hurt the boat or yourself. What we discovered was that for every main current, there was a countercurrent.

The wind might be blowing down the island from the northwest, and that wind could be fairly strong. If you submitted to the ocean 20 or 30 feet off the rocks, you would just blow away down the island, past cove after cove. If you went into a cove, however, into the deep part of the cove, there would be an eddying wind and an eddying current.

All the time you were being taken by the wind and current, you were being rotated so that your visual perception was changing constantly. One minute, you were observing the kelp beds and the open ocean; the next, you were focused on rocks, whitewater, birds, and sea lions, all swirling by. Sometimes you were facing the sun, sometimes away from the sun.

CLOCKWISE FROM TOP LEFT:
Flippy surging at Santa Barbara Island. *Mickey Muñoz*

Malia and *PB&J* rafted up at the Channel Islands. *Mickey Muñoz*

Low tide on Todos Santos Island. *Mickey Muñoz*

In surging, we discovered the countercurrents – that you could actually surge to weather without paddling, by just letting the natural energy of the ocean move you. Instead of fighting against the wind and the main current, you could place yourself in a countercurrent and surge your way to weather. That reaffirmed a lot of the past experiences in my life. What I discovered was that my life has been about living in the countercurrent. I've spent a lot of time in my life surging to weather.

I kind of like that position. It allows you to look at the mainstream flow that's going by you. All these people who are rushing by are caught in the main current, and they're going so fast that they don't have time to look around and see what's going on around them. From my position, I can jump off into the main current and flow with it for a while when I see something that I like; there's a lot of good stuff in the main current. But having the experience of countercurrent surging lets me get out of the main current anytime I wish and back into the countercurrent where I can rest and refresh my perspective.

It's OK to be in the main current; it's OK to have a watch on; it's OK to take your credit card and plug it in and fly to some exotic destination. If you live in the countercurrent, however, and you surge to weather, you're constantly getting new perspectives, new ideas, new ways of approaching things. And it works.

Red Pumps on Maui

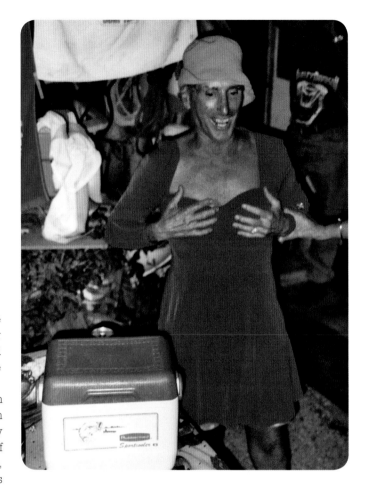

I'm a small-statured surfer, and because I was in the right place at the right time, I was asked to stunt-double for women in surf movies. I'm not a cross-dresser, but I'm not afraid to put women's clothes on. A lot of people are uncomfortable with that.

Fast-forward some years to Hawai'i where I met Jeff Johnson on the North Shore. He had built a boat and sailed it from San Francisco to Hawai'i single-handed. I met him through Flippy Hoffman when Jeff was building a place for Flippy over the top of the house Jeff and his wife Patty were living in. The Eagle's Nest, as it was called, was a tiny single room propped up on four poles over the roof of the existing house. A place for Flippy when he came to the North Shore with a perfect view of Pūpūkea.

Flippy bought more property up near Sunset Point and had Jeff build another house there. Jeff needed help, so I went over and spent half a winter there working with Jeff. Jeff was a really good woodworker, as well as an artist and designer. We surfed, worked, and hung out a lot together.

Jeff got a job remodeling a restaurant in Lahaina. We drove his skiff over from O'ahu and got there on the day they had closed the restaurant and were having a party for the locals. The party was a big deal, so we anchored out and swam in bare-footed holding our tee shirts over our heads and partied with everybody.

I ran into this woman I used to know, and she invited me to go dancing, of course I accepted. "But you've got to have shoes," she said.

"I don't have any shoes," I replied.

"Well, the only extra shoes I have are these red pumps."

"Fine with me," I said, "I'll wear those." So we got ready to go dancing. I was standing there in surf trunks, no shirt, cocktail in hand, and these red two-inch heeled pumps on my feet – a bonus because they made me as tall as her. I looked over while we were talking and saw this big guy looking our way and giving me stink eye. He walked over and strategically placed himself between my friend and me. She introduced me to him and said they were platonic roommates. His name rang a bell, but I couldn't quite place him. I knew he was thinking, "Who is this little fag?"

We talked some more, and he gave me stink eye the whole time. Suddenly, I realized who he was. I had a friend in Laguna who had talked about this guy before. He was one of the original

Navy SEAL guys, a trained killer, bad-ass as they come. My friend had talked about how tough he was and what he had done in Nam. When I realized who I was talking to, I had the advantage. I had done some pretty gnarly stuff too, nothing like this guy – I wasn't a killer – but I had done some pretty serious water stuff, so I started to put him on.

I started talking some pretty good dive stories and underwater encounters with sharks and all this crap. He shook his head, I'm sure he was thinking, "Who is this audacious little shit standing in these red pumps? How dare he?"

Finally he asked, "What's your name again?"

I told him my name and asked, "You don't happen to know a guy by the name of Corky Smith, do you?"

He looked at me and said, "No, shit, I've heard your name. I've heard about you before." He picked me up and gave me a big hug, then said, "All right, let's go dancing.

ABOVE:
Out looking for big waves to ride the 16-footer on: Jeff's skiff at Avalanche with Jeff driving, Flippy in the back corner, and me and Mike Miller in the bow. *Mickey Muñoz Collection*

LEFT:
One of the costume changes at my 60th birthday party. *Mickey Muñoz Collection*

OPPOSITE PAGE:
If the dress fits, wear it: This is an antique red dress, given to me on my 60th birthday to go with the red pumps that I no longer have. *Mickey Muñoz Collection*

Joey and *Hōkūle'a*

Because surfing and sailing are so interconnected, Joey Cabell, a top surfer, got into boats. He and Joe Quigg designed and built *Hōkūle'a*, a 40-foot cat, designed and built for Hawaiian waters: In surfboard terms, that would be like designing a board for the North Shore, compared to designing one for Southern California.

Joey decided to do a big trip to Tahiti and asked me along. I couldn't make the run down, but I joined him to bring the boat back while cruising the Marquesas and Tuamotus. We planned to surf and explore and experience those cultures of the South Pacific. At that time, those islands were not tourist islands; I don't think there were any flights that went there. The only way you could get to them was by boat.

We did a lot of diving, a lot of surfing, and a lot of exploring. We got surf in the Tuamotus at a reefbreak; we didn't get size, but we got quality. We got waves in the Marquesas too. The sailing, of course, was a big part of it.

To join the trip, I flew in to Tahiti and arrived at 1:00 in the morning. I was beat up from the long flight from Los Angeles. Joey met me at the airport. It took forever to get through immigration and customs. They wouldn't inspect my surfboard until the morning, so we had to come back and pick it up later that day. By the time we got to the boat, it was 4:00 or 5:00 in the morning and I couldn't go to bed, so Joey and I talked and caught up on things. The other crewmember, Louie Wake, who I had not met, woke up about 8:00 or 9:00 in the morning.

Hōkūle'a was an interesting boat. After sailing it for a few years, Joey lengthened the hulls by five feet, and that, along with other improvements, made the boat faster and safer. The highly modified Quigg hulls were attached by high-arched fabricated tubes that held a cabin pod. The pod looked like a flattened bubble, centered above the hulls. This low windage and water drag configuration allowed the boat to be sailed fast and efficiently in big seas. The boat's name, *Hōkūle'a* is the Hawaiian name for the star Arcturus, which passes over Hawai'i.

You couldn't stand up in the pod; you had to walk around bent over, but there was headroom when you sat on the settee that went around the perimeter of the pod, and that's where we slept. There were lockers under the settee. The pod was spare, very Spartan, and small, maybe 8 feet wide by 10 feet long. All the other gear was stored in compartments in the hulls that were accessed through a submarine style hatch, which you had to have a crescent wrench to open. The hatches were watertight; when we were sailing, the hulls would go through the waves and had to be submersible. The pod was pretty waterproof too and up high enough that we were above the tops of most waves.

Behind the pod was a little platform, maybe 4 or 5 feet wide and 10 or 12 feet long. That's where you stood or sat outside and drove the boat; the ship's wheel was on the back of the pod. You could get down to the hulls, but it was tedious and tenuous, with no real lifelines. We had jack lines so that if you're really hauling ass you had a harness on, you could clip into the jack lines and get down to the hulls if you needed to get there to do some sort of sail business.

On that first morning onboard, I had just met Louie and was wiped out from the long flight. We still had to buy groceries and other provisions, but Joey had become Captain Joey and was reciting the rules of the vessel. Louie was paying close attention; Louie thought that Joey was God.

He started out with, "This is how you fold your clothes," and he taught us how to fold tee shirts, pants, and shorts so that they would fit into the very small space that Joey had designated for Louie and me to keep our personal effects, along with Joey's guitar. Joey of course, being the captain and owner, had a bigger storage area. Joey went on and on for an hour with this dissertation on how things would be on his boat.

Joey Cabell naviguessing our way from Tahiti to Hawai'i.
Mickey Muñoz

He was near the end of his speech and was talking about a shelf that was over the settee around the front of the pod and below the forward windows that look out. Joey said, ''And nothing is to go up on this dashboard.''

With that, I took my tee shirt off, balled it up and threw it onto the dashboard and replied, ''I cannot live like this.''

Louie went white; he was in total shock that I would talk to God like that. But Joey and I had been friends for so long, I knew I could and he knew I would.

The three of us on the trip had three different personalities, which made the trip very interesting. We each had a different way of thinking and doing things, and there had to be compromise along the way. It was all good-natured. We never got into arguments; we just worked it out.

Ciguatera in the South Seas

We spent several weeks cruising the Tuamotus on Joey's catamaran the *Hōkūle'a*, but we spent most of the time on one island in a big lagoon; just hanging out with the locals, surfing, diving, and fishing. Next, we went to the Marquesas and had a lot of great experiences there. We would anchor close to a village, swim in, and go hiking or check out the village.

We anchored in this one cove that had surf. Joey and I immediately took our boards out and went surfing. The patriarch of the family whose cove it was, paddled out in his outrigger canoe. He wasn't a surfer, but he was a fisherman and a hunter. He brought us some fruit and coconuts and welcomed us to his cove. Our boat fascinated him; it was like a spaceship had landed in front of his home. He was a boat builder and woodcarver, and in the adjoining cove, he was helping build the Marquesian version of a double-hull, 60-foot, voyaging canoe as part of a Polynesian-

wide revival in the traditions and knowledge of the Polynesian voyaging past. It was carved stem to stern – paddles, *ama*, *iako*, everything – by this man whose cove we had anchored in. The canoe was almost complete; they had been building it for some years. He took us to see the canoe, and it was beautiful.

A day or two later, anchored in another cove a mile or so from a village, we had been hiking all day. As we swam out to the boat, I looked down and saw a couple of yummy-looking fish. I climbed aboard the boat, got my spear, went back, and speared a couple of fish. We barbecued them that night, and they were the most delicious fish we had eaten on the whole trip.

At 1:00 in the morning, Louie started throwing up and having diarrhea; 45 minutes later Joey was doing the same. The fish we had just eaten had ciguatera. For some reason, it didn't affect me as radically, but they were both sick-sick. Louie was so bad that the next morning he told us his will, what he was giving to his wife and the rest of his family . . . he thought he was going to die.

The symptoms were awful: Eighty-degree water felt like 40 degrees; your eyes felt like they were full of sand; they weren't

comfortable open or shut. Your whole body tingled, and you could feel the poison surging through your bloodstream. Your tongue and throat were tingling and numb. It was really apparent that you were poisoned. It was horrible.

Normally when we caught fish on the reefs, we would go to the village, tell the locals where we caught the fish, and ask if the fish was OK to eat. The villagers knew. But we were really tired the day we caught the fish that poisoned us, and the one day we didn't bother to ask, we got sick.

Ciguatera is in the algae on the reef. When the system is upset by a storm or some other ecological catastrophe, that algae becomes more prolific and gets caught in the food chain. If the ecological upset is only in one cove, that cove will be contaminated, and a half-mile away the next cove will be just fine. The islanders know pretty much where it's good and bad.

Because I didn't get hit as hard, it was up to me to deal with Louie and Joey. I managed to get the anchor up and the boat going. We sailed the boat 25 miles across a channel to an island where our sailing guide said there could be a doctor. We anchored in the main cove, and the first person who came out to see us was an English doctor who had been cruising in the area. He had just been in to see the French doctor, the only doctor on the island, and coincidentally, they had talked about ciguatera, so he knew something about it.

When we described the symptoms, he diagnosed it right away. He took Joey and Louie in his inflatable to the shore and then managed to get them to hike a couple of miles inland to the local doctor. Louie spent the night there on an IV. Joey came back to the boat. The next day we got Louie; there wasn't much they could do for him other than rehydrate him and give him vitamins. Fortunately, after being rehydrated Louie felt a little better. The doctor's advice was no fish products or by-products, including canned fish or packaged fish, for at least 30 days. That was going to be a challenge on a sailing trip across an ocean full of fish.

TOP TO BOTTOM:
The family patriarch, whose cove we are anchored in, invited us to a dinner of roast wild goat. Marquesas. *Mickey Muñoz*

Joey weaves a palm frond hat. *Mickey Muñoz*

The whole canoe had this elaborate carving on it, from stem to stern, keel to gunwale. Marquesas. *Mickey Muñoz*

OPPOSITE PAGE:
Louie checks out a Marquesan anchorage from the bow of *Hōkūle'a*. *Mickey Muñoz*

Fun and Games

After a week or so of recovery from ciguatera, we got our act together and prepared to set off for Hawai'i. There was one little village market, the size of a closet, but it did stock spam and beer, so I bought six Hinano beers. At that time, Joey and Louie were practicing Seventh Day Adventists, and they had stopped drinking. Joey asked what I was going to do with the beer and reminded me we didn't have any refrigeration. I told him I would stash them in the bilge and that they might come in handy later. We finished provisioning and took off for Hawai'i.

Joey called his wife before we departed and gave her our schedule; our onboard communications were fairly rudimentary. We had a VHF radio, which is line of sight, usually only good for about 25 miles. Our short-wave radio had broken, and we had no way to fix it. Our only other mode of communication besides the VHF was an EPIRB (Emergency Position Indicating Radio Beacon) – a signaling device only to be activated in dire emergency. It sends out a distress signal to ships and airplanes in the area. We were crossing what probably at that time was one of the least traveled routes on the planet. Even if we activated the EPIRB signal it would be sheer luck if it were picked up.

We left the Marquesas and were having a glorious sail – we had the spinnaker up and plenty of wind. On the third day out, the wind mellowed, and we slowed down a bit. We still had the spinnaker up, and to pass the time, we played a game.

On Joey's catamaran there is a bridle that connects the forestay – the wire that holds the mast from falling backward – to the bows. The bridal forms a V shape between the forestay and the bows, the center of which is about 15 feet off the water. For fun, we climbed the bridle to the forestay, dove into the spinnaker and slid off into the water. We had a line stretched between the transoms – you had to time it just right – that you could grab when you came up, flip onto your stomach and you would be bodysurfing behind the boat. Then you would pull yourself over to the side and climb up on the boat. Since there was no reason to have clothes on in the middle of the Pacific, we were doing this naked.

I had done it three times, and on the fourth time I mistimed it just a tad and came up in front of the fairing pod that housed the

The bridle made a great diving platform, even at anchor.
Mickey Muñoz Collection

outboard motor. I didn't want to hit it, so I ducked under again. Right then the boat caught a little gust of wind and a little wave and surged forward. I came back up and put my hands up in the air and *tick*, the line stretched between the transoms hit my fingertips and was gone.

I was naked, 800 miles from the Marquesas, 1,200 miles from Hawai'i, and watching the boat sail away with a big spinnaker up – that's a lot of sail area – and only two guys to deal with it.

As I watched the boat sailing away, I felt this little line going by and remembered we had a log line out. The log line was an eighth-inch line with a torpedo-shaped instrument – called a fish – with a prop at the end of it. The prop spun and told you how far and how fast you were going – that was our speed indicator. I grabbed that line, and it smoked through my fingers. There was no way I could hold on, but I knew the fish was coming up. As soon as that fish hit my hands I clamped on to it like a vise and it pulled me out of the water and I ended up bodysurfing behind the boat. Luckily the line didn't break.

I felt like I was bait, like a big old trolling lure. Joey and Louie finally got the spinnaker down and stopped the boat and I gladly swam swiftly to the boat.

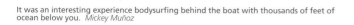

It was an interesting experience bodysurfing behind the boat with thousands of feet of ocean below you. *Mickey Muñoz*

Dismasted

Joey has two speeds: He's either wide open or he's asleep. While sailing, he wanted to go as fast as possible, and he always pushed his boat. On the trip, I wanted to enjoy the ocean – I love going fast, too – but I didn't think it was necessary to break any speed records. I had hoped the trip would slow down a little bit. I got my wish in a way that I hadn't foreseen.

One night on the trip back, we got into a rainsquall. Previously, we had locked the rotating part of the mast in a fore and aft position because it was a hassle to have it rotating. It wasn't the right thing to do; the mast was designed to rotate to present its strongest shape to the line of most stress. But anyway, the squall was coming, and I was on the helm. It was 3:00 in the morning, when all wonderful things happen, pitch black. I checked the compass, I checked the spinnaker, I left the helm for 10 seconds to reach into the pod to grab my foul weather gear and put it on. I came back and looked down at the compass and saw I was on course.

I looked up at the spinnaker and it looked like it was luffing by the lee; the wind had clocked. I didn't want to jibe, so I turned the boat into the wind and ended up luffing, stalling the boat by going head to wind with the spinnaker up, which is strictly a downwind sail. The rudders had lost effectiveness because there was no longer any flow across them. We were dead in the water and starting to go backward. I tried to reverse the helm, but the spinnaker was now blowing back into the shrouds and mast. About the only thing we could do now was to release the halyard and try to wrestle the spinnaker down and get the sail and boat under control.

It was dark, raining pretty hard, and blowing 15 to 18. Louie was standing next to me at the helm; Joey was out on one of the hulls looking up at the rigging and wondering what to do. All of a sudden we heard a loud *crack*. "Oh, shit." The mast was breaking, but I looked up, and it seemed OK, so I thought it must have been the halyard that parted.

That was the last thought I had; the next thing I knew I was being hammered to the deck. The 60-foot, heavy-duty aluminum mast had broken near the bottom third, and the top two-thirds was blown straight back and had hit me on the neck and shoulder and driven me to the deck, face down and out cold.

Joey, who was hanging on to a mast shroud on the starboard hull, went into the water. Louie saw the mast coming and hit the deck before the mast could hit him. The mast, the boom, the sails, and all the rigging went into the water and started banging against one of the hulls. They got to me and asked if I was OK. I was barely conscious and disoriented; they had to tell me where we were and what we were doing. I couldn't feel or move my fingers or toes. I was paralyzed from my neck down. I told them, "Don't move me; I think my neck is broken."

They covered me with a blanket and left me face down on the deck. They had plenty of other things to deal with: The broken mast, boom, and sails, all connected by the stays were over the side, and with the wave action there was a chance they could hole the boat.

They finally got things tied off and under enough control to get back to me. By then, my fingers and toes were tingling, and I was starting to get some feeling and movement in them. I started

After we got dismasted, things slowed way down. Joey (l) and Louie (r) in front of our jerry-rigged mast. *Mickey Muñoz*

thinking that I might not be totally paralyzed, but I worried my neck was broken and any adverse movement could do me in. I was still face down on the deck in the rain – cold and scared. I told them to get the cutting board, brace my head and neck with it, and get me inside. They got me as comfortable as possible and went back out to try and get all the gear back on deck.

By midmorning, they had gotten the wreckage pretty much together. They had lashed one piece of the mast on one side of the pod and the other piece on the other side. They had gotten the sails together and rolled up.

By late that afternoon, I had to go to the bathroom. I figured I would rather die than be a baby in their arms, going to the bathroom while they held me. I told them to get me up, and I

would take it from there. So they propped me up, and I managed to stagger to my feet and get myself over to the side to do my business. Then I got my camera and started taking pictures of what I could.

I still thought my neck was broken, but at least I could move around a little bit. I didn't try turning my head. We debated on whether or not to activate the EPIRB, but in the end, we decided that I wasn't dying-dying, so we didn't set it off. But we did have to come up with a strategy to get home.

We only had three or four hours of fuel. That would get us 20 or 25 miles and that would be it, so we wouldn't be motoring home; we had to sail there. We couldn't contact anybody because there was no one to contact and no way to do it. We

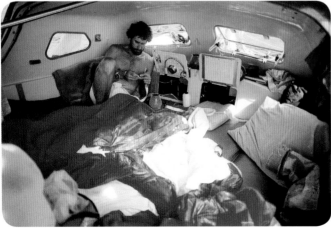

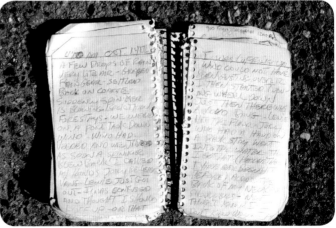

had gone from a highly efficient catamaran sailing at speed to stopped. To top it off, we were just entering the doldrums where the wind quits.

We delved into our collective experience of boat building and engineering. Louie is really smart engineering-wise and had been around boats a long time, and Joey had helped build the boat. Between all of us, we figured out a plan. We rigged lines on the boom and raised it where the mast had been; the boom was 16 feet long and had a bunch of rigging on it that we could use for the sails. We then took the mainsail, turned it sideways, and rigged the foot of it to the boom. The luff of the sail became the foot and ran parallel to the deck. We put a block on the end of the longest piece of broken mast that was sticking out past the stern and used that to run the sheet line through and forward to the cockpit. We then had a low, long sail that we could control and shape well enough to sail to weather. Next, we rigged the jib sideways like the main, and then we had enough sail area to move the boat. We were back in business!

The next few days we rigged a water catchment system, took stock of our food and water, and fabricated a downwind sail out of the torn spinnaker. We took the largest half of the spinnaker and tied lines on it where we thought appropriate and set it. While it was up we made a drawing of it. The next several days we sewed it into a new spinnaker similar to a square sail. It had to be good enough to a last 1,000 miles or more.

That configuration moved the boat when there was wind. Ironically enough, we had about 30 days of dry food and emergency food, but we couldn't eat any fish, so our emergency fishing gear was useless. We were in a survival mode.

The first three days after we left the Marquesas we sailed over 900 miles; after the dismasting and jerry-rigging, it took us five days to get a little over 100 miles. We had slowed down!

That was a real change of pace for us adrenaline junkies, and it allowed us to talk more. Those Hinano beers I had bought back in the Marquesas suddenly became very sacred. It was amazing what we talked about. We would have these afternoon EST-like sessions; we talked story, played guitar, and sang. We talked about our lives, where we were going, and what we were doing.

I can't remember how long it took us, but we finally got back in the trade winds and started making some good mileage again. Louie was the first to see land; he spotted the volcano on the Big Island and jumped up and down with excitement. Both Joey and I looked at the volcano, then turned back around and said in unison, "Oh, shit, we're here already."

We were totally into just living on the ocean. I don't know how else to explain it.

We radioed out on the VHF; Joey talked to his wife, and she was greatly relieved as she had sent a plane out to try and find us; we were way late. We motored into Hilo Harbor – we hadn't used any of our fuel yet – and pulled up to the Coast Guard dock and gave them our report. We went into Hilo and had dinner.

The next day we did our laundry, and late that afternoon, we got back on the boat and started to head back out. The Coast Guard was taken aback. "Where are you going? What are you doing?"

"Oh, we're sailing the boat to O'ahu," we replied.

"You can't go like that."

"We just sailed 1,200 miles like this, we think we can make it." And laughing, out we went.

It took us several more days to get to O'ahu. We wanted the extra days at sea. When we got to Waikiki, this big flotilla of boats came out. We weren't ready for all of that. It was a huge culture shock to get back.

CLOCKWISE FROM TOP:
Joey navigating with a sextant. *Mickey Muñoz*

Pages from my log. *Mickey Muñoz*

Joey resewing the torn spinnaker for its new configuration on our jerry-rigged mast. *Mickey Muñoz*

Hot and Glassy

After the winter I surfed Waimea, I went back to Hawai'i every winter for about the next 10 or 15 years. I wasn't a big-wave hound, but I would take it on if it happened. It was probably due to a lot of peer pressure and a reputation for riding big waves. I can't say I loved it, but I was a good enough waterman that I could pull it off reasonably well. Sometimes though, I was really afraid. I would find myself in really big-wave situations that were foolish and ask myself, "What am I doing out here? This is stupid!"

One day, a friend and I walked from Waimea to Pipeline along the beach. We sat in the sand at Pipeline and watched people surf. It was about 8 to 10 feet, a beautiful perfect day, and there were 50 of the best surfers in the world out there competing for waves. After 45 minutes, I turned to my friend and said, "You know this is the first time I've been able to sit on the beach and really enjoy watching others surf without feeling like I have to go out."

My friend didn't really understand what I meant until I started explaining myself. I think it was at that moment that I realized that I didn't have to prove anything to anybody – to myself in particular. And that I really liked hot and glassy, 4- to 8-foot point-surf waves, giggling and laughing and having fun with my friends – not constantly being in high-stress situations. That's where I surfed the best and had the most fun. Surfing had always been fun for me, but from then on, it took on a different meaning. Of course, I still challenge myself and "hang it out" because that's living at a high level.

That realization was a real breakthrough for me. I didn't have to go out in the water. I didn't have to force myself. I was happy to be on the beach and just watch really high-level surfing and not have to be out in the water doing it. Throughout my surfing career, I have enjoyed the adrenaline rush – that's a part of surfing for me – but I realized I didn't have to seek it constantly.

CLOCKWISE FROM TOP:
You come out of the water chilled and lie down on the beach, snuggle in, and pull warm sand up to your chest. It's a time to talk story with your friends and watch surfers in the water – it's as much a part of surfing as the surfing itself. *Mickey Muñoz Collection*

Hot and glassy describes different things: On a boat, it's a hot and glassy cove, no wind, no current, very little wave action, ideal anchoring, and just hanging out with no stress and no worries about dragging anchor . . . it's a time to kick back. *Mickey Muñoz*

On the nose, and hot and glassy in Anglet, France. A side benefit, uniquely French, is stunningly beautiful naked women on the beach. *Bill Parr*

The Present Is Just Layers of the Past

I have an artist friend I dearly love – Michael Logan. I have these acrylic paintings he did of Trestles. I've ridden that wave a zillion times, and though Michael isn't a surfer, he captured that break on canvas perfectly.

Michael and I were down in Baja at a point south of the Halfway House. He had leased some property and put a trailer and a little shack on it. The Halfway House, as the name implies, was halfway between Tijuana and Ensenada. At that time, there was nothing else between the two towns except for a few little fish camps.

I was fascinated watching Michael paint with acrylics; I had never watched anyone paint before. Painting with acrylics is a very fast process, unlike oils where you have to let the paint dry before you layer over with more paint, acrylics dry so fast you can overpaint almost immediately.

We stood on the bluff looking north along the cliff line. The Halfway House was on the right with the mountains behind it. Down to the left was the ocean with waves coming in on the rocks – breaking and receding – and a little bit of sand scalloped in a small cove.

Michael started off with this blank canvas, and he started splashing a neutral color on the canvas with a big, wide brush, and in a pattern I couldn't make any sense out of. I didn't have a clue what he was doing. Next, he mixed up a color and started filling in more details and suddenly the bluff started to take shape. With some of that same color, he started to sketch in the mountains. Then he started to paint in the Halfway House in a darker color. Next he painted the ocean on the other side and then some of the ocean colors went back into the fields and into the mountains. Then he started painting in the sky and clouds, and all the colors got distributed around.

I watched how he did it and how the painting grew, but what I was really watching was his progression painting the ocean. He painted so fast. A wave would come in and break and rush up through the rocks and onto the beach and then recede back down. It might form a little counterwave that wove its way back down through the rocks. There was a current formed by the water that was higher on the beach and the water flowing down the coast before the northwest winds. He painted those waves as they broke and how each wave looked at the instant in time that it was affected by the counterwave coming off the beach.

Then he went back and used that color back somewhere else in the painting and left the ocean alone for several minutes. Later, as another wave broke, he came back and overpainted how he saw the ocean five minutes later. Each time he painted a wave, it was different because each set, each wave, each pattern had been affected by the conditions that occurred prior to it.

When he stopped painting, the ocean was alive. The waves were breaking and receding in the painting, because of all those layers of paint. My observation of the process it took to get those layers of paint on the canvas gave me a perspective on life that I hadn't seen before: Our present is made up from layers of our past. We have all these wavelets and currents and countercurrents and winds in our lives. Our present is built from our past. We are built by all of our friends and our experiences.

Michael knew that intuitively, and that's the way he painted.

Michael Logan painting at the Halfway House in Baja. *Mickey Muñoz Collection*

Surfing Hobie Cats in Hawai'i

Phil Edwards and me surfing a Hobie 16 at Outside Sunset. Hawai'i.
Mickey Muñoz Collection

Phil Edwards and I had fantasized about riding big waves on a catamaran. We had surfed Poche shorebreak, where the Hobie Cat was born, but we didn't know the limits of how big a wave we could ride. In those days one of the problems with some big-wave boards was that they would load up and slow you down midway down the wave face pitching you over the nose of your board if you weren't in perfect trim. That same phenomena that allowed you to nose-ride – that belly and curve in the tail that sucks the tail down – when shaped into the nose, worked against you on big waves: Nose rocker and too much belly in the nose got sucked down in the water and would stop the board if you were in the wrong position.

We didn't know whether the same thing would happen with a catamaran going fast on a big wave. The result wouldn't be good: possibly wrapping you around the stainless steel rigging cables, getting tangled in the sheets, sails, or trampoline, or banging you against the rudders or hulls. There was a lot more to deal with than getting pitched off your board.

Phil and I talked about sailing a Hobie Cat in Hawai'i and riding waves there. Hobie Alter thought it would be a good promotional tool for the catamarans if we wanted to do it. Hobie Cat arranged to get a couple of boats over there, and they were prepared to write one off if we wrecked it. Phil and I had sailed a lot together, but we practiced riding bigger and bigger waves here, although there wasn't anything in Southern California anywhere near the size of a wave at Sunset Beach on the North Shore.

Phil and I had both built our own boats 10 years prior to this endeavor, and we'd spent a lot of time together on boats in some pretty exciting conditions. When I was working for Carter Pyle building P-Cats, Phil had built a 20-foot outrigger that he kept up in Newport. One day, there was one of these Santa Ana winds where everything turned black from the dust, and the wind was howling – gusting to 40 or 50 knots. We decided we were going to sail Phil's outrigger. We left the beach and immediately wiped out and broke some gear. We took the pieces to Carter's shop, fixed them, and went back to repeat our performance.

Carter, Phil, and I took off from the beach at 19th Street, and headed down the channel toward the turning basin. Right from the start, we were totally out of control, going 20 plus knots easy. We got to the end of the channel, and it was blowing even harder. We had our *ama* on the windward side and were trying to keep it down. The canoe's nose was being pressed down into the water by the pressure of the wind on the sail. That pulled the rudder out of the water, so we had to steer with the sail, but we had the sail out as far as it would go. We were all screwed up and rounding up into the wind.

We went across the opening of the turning basin, and there in front of us sat a 60-foot powerboat with its stern facing us. On the stern was a teak swim deck with big stainless steel tubing around it, and we were headed for it at mach speed. The *ama* came up and my reflex was to go out on it to keep it down. We should have just let the canoe turn over and dumped it right then and there. My reflex to go out on the *ama* won out, but I missed it. Because there was no net over the big opening between the hull and the *ama*, I went in the water. The canoe kept going and center-punched the swim platform.

Phil stuffing a bow while surfing his Hobie 14 at Poche. *Mickey Muñoz Collection*

After that Carter and Phil always accused me of jumping off the boat when things got sketchy. My version was I didn't jump off the boat; I was going for the *ama*. But whatever happened, happened.

Even though Phil hadn't been to Hawai'i or riding big waves much in the years before our big-wave catamaran surfing adventure, we were ready to go when we got sponsored. We were going to try to surf a Hobie cat on as big a wave as we could find on O'ahu's North Shore.

I fantasized about how it would happen; in my wildest dreams I thought it would be great if we got in this giant barrel

and Phil jumped off the boat so I could tease him like he and Carter teased me for jumping off the outrigger canoe back in Newport. Well, it didn't quite happen that way.

It was a pretty fair sized day at Sunset, the Hawaiians would have called it 5 feet, but in California we would have called it 15 to 18 feet – some good-sized waves. The wind was blowing 25 knots plus; there was plenty of wind and we had our main sail reefed. We reached outside and then turned back in and were able to catch waves on the outside, outside reefs, where you would tow in these days. The waves weren't really breaking out there, but we could take off on the crumbling bumps and ride them till they reformed inside where you would normally surf. We rode two or three waves but pulled out before the inside.

Then came this one wave, a good-sized wave, which we took off on outside and rode it all the way to the inside takeoff spot. As we got to the inside, the wind shifted to straight off-shore. We no longer had the wind to assist us as much as we had outside. We weren't reaching anymore; we were almost dead into it. We managed to get inside and somehow make the wave, but after we got out of the wave, we were stalled right in the impact zone with our bows pointed straight in.

Right then a set came, not a big wave, but a good 8- to 10-foot, double-overhead wave, and we were right where it was going to break. Phil dove off the back end of the boat and under the wave. I looked at the wave and thought we might be OK. I grabbed the tiller and back crossbar and put my head down, like I was duck diving into the wave. The wave broke over the boat and washed me off the back of the boat. Somehow I managed to hang on and the boat didn't pearl. The boat ended up riding the wave with me behind hanging on to the crossbar.

I managed to pull myself back onto the boat when the wave backed off a little. I steered the boat all the way up onto the beach and stepped off onto the sand. Phil was still out in the water; a guy had to paddle out to give him fins so he could swim in. It didn't happen quite the way I had fantasized it would, but at least it stopped Phil from teasing me about jumping off his boat.

The Catalina
Paddleboard Race

A friend of mine knew a woman named Peggy and said to me, "I think I know someone you might really like." Peggy wanted to learn how to windsurf, and my friend thought I could teach her.

Our first date was on *Malia*; our second date was on *Malia* too. I took Peggy across to Catalina Island to meet some of her friends. I was going over to paddle in the Catalina paddleboard race. It was one of the roughest crossings I have ever had: I was scared shitless. It was blowing out of the north averaging 20 to 25 and gusting to 30 knots. It was a small-craft warning, and it was shitty. My friend, Kent, who loaned me the paddleboard, came along to drive my boat back as an escort for me. He had just come off a 34-day fast, and was still recovering and not at full strength. Peggy didn't have a clue about sailing, but she was there ready, strong, and willing to help.

It was so bad that half the escort boats never made it over to escort the paddlers. Peggy hooted, laughed, and giggled the entire way across. She just loved it. I said to myself "Oooh, this be a keeper."

We dropped Peggy off in Avalon to meet her friends, and then we had another 15 miles to go to get to the Isthmus where the race started the next morning. We got there in the cold and dark, and the tiny cove was slammed with boats.

One of the things with anchoring *Malia* was you had to be a weather vane to the wind at all times; otherwise, any kind of cover you put would become like a spinnaker and drag you around. Because it was so crowded I ended up putting down three anchors – diving with my tank at 10:00 at night – so we could rotate around in a small diameter circle .

I got back up at 4:30 or 5:00 to eat some food and do some stretching, yoga, and meditation before the race started at 6:00.

Kent was a little hesitant about taking the boat out on his own, so I got the anchors up and stowed, and the boat prepped for sea – tent down and all the camping and sleeping gear off the deck – and out of the anchorage. I motored *Malia* out a half mile off the beach, and then had to paddle back in for the start.

Kent wouldn't let me put knee wells in his 16-footer, which meant I had to paddle it prone the whole way. That's a long way to paddle prone – I was in shape for prone paddling from all my surfing, but it's nice to be able to get to your knees to change up the muscle groups and body position. The board had a lot of rocker, which would have been good in really rough conditions, but it had way more rocker than it needed for the residual bump that was left over on the morning of race day.

The race started. We took off, and Kent came over to me after the race officials let the escort boats into the pack. I was reasonably competitive for the first three hours, the real hot leaders were pretty much gone, but I was in the pack and doing well enough. Then I hit the wall, got the deep shakes, and lost my coordination. I was really screwed up.

I had made some smoothies and other stuff to drink on the way, but because Kent was recovering from his fast, he had drunk them. I had a dry wetsuit on the boat that I put on, and Kent had some dates that I ate. I had been really good about drinking water the whole time, and after eating some dates I started to feel my strength coming back. I warmed back up and started paddling again. By the time I got to the finish, I had my second wind. Just finishing the crossing was a huge deal for me; I had wanted to do it for a long time.

Midchannel in the Catalina paddleboard race.
Mickey Muñoz Collection

Lucky
To Be Surfers

I was learning to windsurf a number of years ago in Hawaiʻi. Windsurfing was a sport I was suited for. I'm a surfer, I'm a sailor, I'm an ocean person: It was the perfect sport for me. It wasn't that easy to learn, though.

During my humbling learning curve, I got good enough to go out in wind and waves that you couldn't do as a rank beginner. I was just good enough for a friend to take me to Diamond Head. We stood on the bluff and looked down on 75 to 100 windsurfers darting in and out with their colorful sails, all screaming along in the 20-knot trade winds. I looked over and saw this little group of surfers on an obscure peak off to the side that had inconsistent surf. They just sat around waiting for waves. "God, that looks dull," I thought to myself.

We schlepped our gear down the bluff trail to the beach, and after a half hour of rigging, mucking around, and getting our gear together, we went windsurfing. I spent the next two hours just barely surviving: I tried to stay off the reefs, jibe when I could, and do water starts. Back at the beach, we derigged our gear and carried it back up the bluff: It was a full day coming and going.

Several days later, I was out on the North Shore. It was summertime, and normally the North Shore doesn't break in the summer. I was staying right at Pūpūkea, and Pipeline is only a couple hundred yards away. Pipeline didn't have a soul out, but there were some four footers coming through, and the sun was going down over Kaʻena Point. I paddled out, sat there, and looked around.

Windsurfing at Diamondhead, I didn't have a chance to look at anything; I was in pure survival mode. That day at Pipeline, sitting out there alone in one of the most beautiful places on earth and getting some fun waves while watching the sun go down, I realized how lucky I was to be a surfer.

It was at that moment I realized that surfing wasn't really the ride; it was the process of getting there. It was the ride to the ride that was the important thing.

Jeff Hakman at Pipeline. *Mickey Muñoz*

Photography
and the Packrat

I'm a packrat; I've got boxes and boxes of slides, boxes and boxes of print images, and hard drives full of digital images. I save everything. It made it hard to do this book; there was just so much to choose from. I was worried I would miss out on a great shot to include or leave out one of my dear friends.

I even have my original copy of *Surfer* that came out in 1960 when I was 23. I'm not good at taking care of things; Peggy keeps me in line in that area. Once they became antiques, suddenly this *Surfer* got to be worth some bucks. Peggy told me, "You better take care of this." "Yes dear."

I kept all my issues of *Surfer*, up to a point. I took *National Geographic* too, and there's not enough room in the world to stack all the *Surfer*, *The Surfer's Journal*, *Longboard*, *Ski*, *Snowboard*, *Multihulls* and *Diver* magazines; somewhere you have to stop. I probably had every issue of *Surfer* through the '70s, maybe into the '80s, and then I stopped.

Photography is a different story. I got into it because I put myself in places that a lot of people weren't. With the advent of digital photography, everybody who has a cell phone has a camera, and the point-and-shoots are so small there's no excuse to not have one. When I started taking photos, it wasn't that way.

My first camera was a Kodak that I got in the early '60s; I don't really remember. Toward the end of the '60s, I got more serious about it. I hated all the paraphernalia that went with it, and could never afford the Nikons or Canons. In the '70s, Olympus came out with some of the first affordable high-quality and compact equipment, although they would be considered bulky by today's standards. That was the first real camera, lenses, motor drives, and strobes that I got.

One of my real good friends and gurus, Bev Morgan, who was quite a photographer, turned me on to the original Nikonos camera. It was machined out of solid stock bronze and later out of aluminum solid stock. Because of the simplicity of the lenses on those, they took very high-quality images, but you had to manually set everything. There was a lot of trial and error for me with that camera; I wasn't a real anal technician.

I wasn't really a photographer; I was more of a documenter. My theory was if I have a camera where I am, and nobody else has one, and I get a shot, even if it has some flaw, at least I've got the shot. I ended up carrying a camera with me just about everywhere I went; I wanted to document for myself all my sailing and surfing adventures. *Surfer* magazine did buy some of my shots, and after a while, it started to almost pay for the equipment, but I never considered myself a professional photographer; it was just part of what I did.

The other thing I really love about photography is how it changes your perspective of things. I love that concept because it is kind of like the concept of surging. You are relaxed and at the mercy of the elements – the current, wind and waves – and you allow yourself to flow with those elements, rotating and moving through space. At the same time, because of the camera, you are constantly aware of your visual frame of reference changing. You are in the flow but also aware of the flow.

The use of different camera lenses can also change your perspective. You can use a telescopic lens that gives you an eagle's eye view of some distant object, use a wide-angle lens and fill the frame with a panoramic of a coastline, or go to a macro lens and shoot a grain of sand as if it were a giant granite boulder. Obviously, your perspective has changed, and the way you look at sand has changed.

You see that sand is made up of ground up seashells and granite and that dirt is made up of crumbling leaves and wood and all this other stuff that is degrading. You no longer pick up dirt and think it's just brown finely ground rock; you know it's more than that.

You start looking at colors the way an artist sees them: Green is not just green; it's yellow and blue and red. It's all these other colors mixed together that gives you the illusion of green. That's what you get when you start to probe with different lenses. You see that, and it heightens the experience. It trains your eye and brain to look at things differently.

The Evolution
of Speed

The *paipo* boards from Hawai'i influenced me the most as I started to understand, through repetition and observation, more about surfboard design and what really works in the water.

Paipos, made from plywood veneers, were almost triangular in shape with the front point of the triangle tipped up and the two opposing corners tipped down like fins. They had pretty flat bottoms and were planing vehicles. They were very radical and very efficient. You had to take off really late because you were swimming into the wave, but once they got up and planing, they were fast.

Proof of that speed could be seen at Waimea Bay on big days when Buzzy Trent was riding one of his 11-foot, radical, pin-tailed guns. He would drop into these horrible maws and aim for the bottom; if he could make it to the bottom, he could make the wave. Nobody on a surfboard was going faster, deeper, or bigger than he was at the time. Those *paipo* guys would drop in after Buzzy would be a third of the way down the face of the wave; once they got up to speed, they would rocket by him like he was standing still.

The problem with standing on something like that, though, was that the board was going airborne. At that time, to go airborne on a board and still maintain your balance was not easy. The boards were bigger and heavier and not as maneuverable; if you did go airborne and you didn't land perfectly, you went down. On *paipo* boards, the rider was prone, hanging onto the board, and just rocketing.

The next influence, George Greenough, came a little later. I was at Rincon on a really good day, and it was the first time I saw somebody make a full carving S-turn without breaking the plane. Again, he was on his knees holding onto the board, still able to go airborne and maintain, but he could carve that board while he was going really fast.

Simmons had the same vision with his boards – concave bottoms, turned down rails in back, and twin fins – they were ahead of their time. The *paipo* board and the Greenough spoon were both basically the nose and tail of a Simmons board stuck together. Shorten the Simmons board from 10 feet to 4 or 5 feet, and you've got what Greenough and the *paipo* guys were riding.

Long and narrow was not necessarily better than short and wide. Shaping is all about balancing control and speed. We love to go fast; speed is your friend but only if you can control it. So you juggle and balance those two factors when you are shaping. I found it fascinating then, and I still do.

Waves in Hawai'i have plenty of speed. The wave train is moving faster than the coast here, because Hawai'i doesn't have a continental shelf. Our bottom gradually gets shallower and shallower, and the wave train slows down earlier. By the time it gets to the point where it can trip and break, it's slowed down considerably compared to Hawai'i, where waves come in from very deep water. There are places in California like Black's Beach or Hollywood by the Sea that have a trench or underwater canyon. The wave trains getting into those spots don't slow down as much; it breaks substantially harder and quicker at Hollywood than it does at C Street just up the coast.

Building speed into your boards is no good unless you can control it. You are trying to make the boards fast but controllable. It's a balance that depends on where you are surfing, the type of wave, and how big it is. Up in Ventura, you've got two radically different waves within 10 miles of each other. You would design a different board for Hollywood by the Sea than for C Street.

One of the hot curl boards I built. *Mickey Muñoz*

The next influence came from a trip to Australia in the early '60s when the shortboard thing was just starting. As soon as we landed in Sydney and I met Bob McTavish, we were like long-lost brothers; he really influenced me. McTavish showed me one of his radical concave, vee-bottom boards, and after I came back, I made a bunch of very short boards with wide tails and deep-vee bottoms. Those boards were both faster and more maneuverable than the standard boards of the day.

CLOCKWISE FROM TOP LEFT:
Phil Edwards working on *El Gato*, the catamaran he designed and built. Poche. *Mickey Muñoz*

One of my experiments; I think it ended up as a twin fin. *Mickey Muñoz*

A couple of replica boards I made for Pete Siracusa to hang in his restaurants. San Onofre. *Mickey Muñoz*

A nicely foiled fin. *Mickey Muñoz*

I helped build this composite motorcycle fuselage for a guy that was trying to break the world speed record. He went 120 mph without even getting out of second and was well over 300 by the time he got through the rest of the gears. Bonneville Salt Flats. *Mickey Muñoz*

For every board you shape, your point of view is from the past; it's based on what you've learned in the past. You carry all this stuff in your head – you may not overtly think about it, but it's there – and it's expressed every time you shape a board. My boards are shaped by those encounters with *paipos* and Greenough and McTavish and countless other experiences.

My friend Richard Tracy, an aeronautical engineer who got a PhD in hypersonic aerodynamics at Cal Tech, has been mucking around with foils most of his life. He's pushing 80 now and that's all he's done. A few years back, he made an incredible breakthrough on a foil that he had been working on for 20 plus years. He made a subtle change from the shape he had been doing. That subtle change made a huge difference in the overall design and performance of the plane he is designing and building. That plane can fly supersonically, and also subsonically, with much greater efficiency. It was just a subtle tweak in the shape of the foil. That's why surf-board design and surfing is such a hook for me: If the last wave or the last board shaped was good, the next one is going to be better.

ABOVE AND RIGHT: Bob Montgomery came to me for help building his concept of a jet board. This is what we came up with after a year or so of hard work. With a 40-horse engine and 120 pounds, he got it up to 50 mph and could surf waves with it. He'll get them into production one day. *Mickey Muñoz Collection*

Surfboard Design Evolution

When I started surfing, we surfed the premiere breaks – the pointbreaks and reefbreaks that were the best. We designed and built boards for those places. As the surfing population increased, the beginners to intermediates got pushed out to the edges. Consequently, they started riding waves that we didn't want to ride or had not considered riding. Surfboard shapers then had to evolve surfboard design to accommodate that; as board designers, we designed boards for those fringe breaks. Then that fringe started to dictate what surfing was about.

When those surfers got pushed out on the fringe, they were riding waves that were more prone to closeout. Their concept of surfing became to get as many maneuvers in before the inevitable happened. It became a maneuvering game. Board designs and surfers started leaning in that direction.

The contemporary revolution combined that closeout wave approach with the traditional pointbreak concept of taking off, coming as close to the horns as possible without getting gored and then making the wave. When Kelly Slater came along – I use Kelly as an example because I think he represents the modern approach at a highly developed stage – he was able to combine the beauty, strength, and aesthetics of the pointbreak approach with all of the maneuvers of the beachbreak approach and still complete the dance. He brought out the best of both worlds. That brought surfboard design together back in the middle again; the boards had to maneuver well, but they also had to be able to generate and control the speed.

A quick example of the power of being able to make the wave comes from a contest that Herbie Fletcher put on at Zippers in San Jose del Cabo, in Baja. Herbie had gathered some of the best surfers in the world at that time. Among them were Kelly Slater and Christian Fletcher, two of the first surfers to really explore aerial maneuvers. Zippers has warm water and fast well-shaped waves, it's fun – the kind of wave where surfers could really perform. The best surfers were out there pushing each other. Christian did this amazing, jaw-dropping hop over the rock at Zippers and continued the wave; it just stunned the audience. The crowd hooted and applauded; it was an amazing feat.

Then came the finals; Kelly and Christian went head to head. Christian went higher, and did a little more radical maneuvers, but he didn't complete the dance; he sacrificed the wave for the maneuver. The judges – full disclosure: I was one of the five judges – decided to award the win to Kelly; he did all the maneuvers but also completed the wave. His riding was more rhythmic and more aesthetic in other elements.

There was a giant to-do: Christian flipped out, Herbie flipped out, people were screaming and yelling. At the time, I predicted that Kelly would be the next world champion, and a year or so later he was.

ABOVE:
The board tree. *Jeff Divine*

OPPOSITE PAGE:
Even this sort of maneuver is old hat now. To really be contemporary, it should be upside down and backward with the tail going forward because he's going to land a full 360-degree whatever the hell they call it. Christian Fletcher at Zippers in Cabo San Lucas. *Tom Servais*

Flippy, Surf Honey, and the Mysterious Steaming Coil

Flippy Hoffman, as was his habit, came over one Christmas day to our house. We offered food, and he declined, as he always did, saying he wasn't really hungry, but we could just set the bowl down in front of him. Then like always, he proceeded to eat it. This one Christmas his girlfriend, Susie, had just given him a brand new pair of Ugg boots. While we sat around the table talking and eating, our black pit and lab mix called Surf Honey was nibbling a hole in Flippy's Uggs.

Flippy was pretty tolerant of Surf Honey, because Surf Honey was a smart dog and a really good water dog. Years earlier, I had built these little platforms off the transoms of *Malia* so that you could get out of the water easily and climb up on the boat. I would go down there and stand on the platform to take a leak. The first time we took Surf Honey on the boat, it was a little disconcerting because we wondered where the dog would go to the bathroom. Well, Surf Honey saw me take a leak off those platforms, and the first time he peed on the boat, he went down, put his front paws on the platform, and peed between his front legs into the water; that's how he did it every single time afterward. Flippy loved that; he thought that was a sign of a very smart dog.

That Christmas day after Surf Honey had nibbled all the way through the boots, the hole was discovered, and Peggy and I apologized profusely. Flippy replied, "They were too hot, anyway. They're perfect now."

A group of us loved to go to San Clemente Island. We would adventure around during the day and raft up in the late afternoon. We would usually end up in Pyramid Cove. There would be my boat, Phil Edwards's boat, Flippy Hoffman's, Don Wert's, and other friends' boats. We would all congregate, tie off to each other and party; then between 8:00 and 10:00 – depending on the party – everybody would split off and go re-anchor. The first one to Pyramid Cove was the mother boat, and wouldn't have to move after the party broke up.

Flippy was usually the first one there, so he never had to go off and anchor in the middle of the night after partying. Everybody else did, and Flippy would scream and give us shit while we did. "You wimps, just drop the fuckin' anchor . . . " and on and on.

At night, your perception is not so good; added to that was the partying and the other boats in there. You didn't want to anchor in too close and get caught in the surf, you didn't want to hit the rocks; you didn't want to drag your anchor. Once you put the anchor down, it was a bitch getting all that heavy chain and anchor off the bottom if you needed to reset it.

It was always an issue, and Peggy and I got tired of this constant harassment from Flippy while re-anchoring at night. We would always drag our feet, getting the last rays of the sun, the last dive, or the last exploring or surging, and consequently, we were always usually the last to raft up. So we made sure this one particular day that we got to Pyramid Cove before Flippy. We told Flippy we were just going to go around the corner to another little cove, but instead we anchored in Pyramid: We were the first to anchor, and we were the mother boat.

The raft up happened, and at 10:00 pm everybody split off. Flippy took off, and he went about 50 feet away and dropped his anchor.

I yelled, "Flippy, you're too close."

"What do you mean? We're not gonna hit. And besides, I don't care," he replied.

"Flippy, you're at fault," I yelled back.

"Well, you're fuckin' boat's only angel food cake. I don't care; it's not gonna hurt my boat."

Surf Honey in Baja. *Mickey Muñoz*

I yelled again, "Flippy, you're responsible; you've got to reanchor."

Flippy was famous for putting his head in the sand when the shit hit the fan – he was an ostrich – so he just thought "screw you," and he went to bed. I was pissed off and grumbling; I had a hard time sleeping that night. I didn't want to move; it would have defeated the whole idea of anchoring first – plus, he was responsible. At first light, the sun was still half an hour below the horizon, I felt our boat moving, and I looked up and saw that we had started to rotate together. Slowly but surely, we were going to hit.

Malia was basically a camping boat; Peggy and I slept on deck under a fairing. We could see the boats gradually getting closer while still in bed. It was very light air, so I wasn't worried about any damage, I could just fend off Flippy's boat if we

actually hit gunwales. Flippy's boat got about a half-foot away. Surf Honey got up, stretched, looked around, stepped onto Flippy's boat, and took a giant dump on the aft deck. Then, as the boats started to rotate apart, he stepped back onto our boat, and curled back up in bed.

Peggy and I were dying of laughter; the coil of poop literally steamed on Flippy's back deck as his boat rotated back to its original position 50 feet away. We laughed so hard we woke Flippy up. He saw the pile and thought Surf Honey had swum over there, but we showed him that Surf Honey was perfectly dry and snuggled up in his bed.

"Maybe it was a seagull," we suggested.

Stars & Stripes

Based on my experience building P-Cats with Carter Pyle and building my own boat, I got jobs building and working on other boats: exotic boats, race boats. And I would get to race on them. I had done Mexico, Transpac, and local races, mostly on catamarans and trimarans.

In 1988, the New Zealanders challenged the San Diego Yacht Club for the America's Cup. San Diego Yacht Club got to choose the location. New Zealand got to choose the type of boats. Well, New Zealand came up with their boat for this challenge – a 120-foot monohull – and SDYC fought it in court. The court decision was late in coming and it got down to the wire. San Diego Yacht Club had to respond or lose the cup without even racing for it.

The yacht club had a bunch of powwows and decided that because the New Zealanders had found a loophole in the original America's Cup formula, they would use a loophole too. Using a flaw in the rules that didn't expressly limit the number of hulls, the San Diego Yacht Club decided to build a multihull. They went to some friends of mine who had a good reputation in designing and building multihulls, and that was how we got to build the America's Cup boats for the '88 cup, the 60-foot catamarans called *Stars & Stripes*.

Bob DeLong had a boat shop adjacent to Hobie's "Alley of Broken Dreams." We had to build an extendo on Bob's shop to be able to build these boats. Bob hired me to help fabricate the hulls. Dennis Conner gave us a blank check to kick New Zealand's ass with a catamaran. The boats were 60 feet long and 30 feet wide, so they took up a big footprint. We built two boats, each with different rigs. One had a hard rig that was sort of like an airplane wing. The other one we built had a soft rig, which was a more conventional-looking Marconi rig. Even the soft rig had a 103-foot carbon wing mast. The big wing for the hard rig was 113 feet and articulated. When it was in its wind slot, it was unbeatable.

We ended up finishing two complete 60-foot boats in three months and one week. We did the R&D on the composite structures, built the mockups and the molds, we built the accessories like the cross tubes, daggerboards, and rudder controls. There are a ton of details on boats

I took this shot from 103 feet up the mast. To give you an idea of scale, that's a 40-foot catamaran docked behind *Stars & Stripes*, which was 60 feet long: In boats everything goes up exponentially. *Mickey Muñoz*

Mickey, Thanks for all your help! Dennis Conner

that make it an endless task. We worked 24/7 to get those boats done on time and delivered to San Diego.

The day the last hull went on the truck to San Diego, we broke out the champagne. Then we got a call from Tom Omohundro who said he needed a couple of our best guys up there; he was behind on the mast for the boats. John Wake and I slugged down our glasses of champagne, got our grinding clothes on, drove to Costa Mesa, and got back to work. I worked all the rest of the day and all that night. I got home in time to kiss Peggy good morning as she was headed out for work. I got a few hours of sleep and went back to Costa Mesa and worked another 24 hours. I went back home, packed my bags, and immediately left for San Diego and spent the next three months there putting in 16- to 18-hour days working on and sailing the boats.

I was on the backup and support crew for the Cup. It was an adventure. At that time, those were probably the fastest two sailboats in the world. Crossing an ocean on one would have been a trick, but for all-out, flat-water speed, I don't think they could have been beaten. They were designed to triple wind speed. We were clocked at over 18 knots in 6 knots of wind: The ocean wasn't even whitecapping, and we were going 18 knots. Even today, that's pretty good.

Dennis always wanted modifications. We would sail all day, which sounds really great, but in reality it's hard work. At the end of the day, the rock stars – the highly paid, professional sailors – went home to shower, have a nice dinner, and go to sleep. We enlisted swine would take off our sailing clothes, put on our fiberglass grinding clothes, and go to work all night so the rock stars could step onto a better boat in the morning. The cats dueled against each other every day.

Dennis, of course, was on the hard rig, the one he was going to race. He had all the rock stars on his boat. I was on the enlisted swine team, and two days before the Cup, we beat them by over two minutes, which is a big differential. Dennis wouldn't speak to us for days after that duel.

Oracle, a multihull in the 2010 America's Cup proved the multihull with a hard wing again. It was hugely efficient. After 20 years, they had perfected the articulating wing and the electronics and controls that make it easier to keep the flow attached, its about flow and power control. I watched the Cup races on my computer; at one time I saw 37 on *Oracle's* knot meter, and it was barely whitecapping.

TOP: Dennis was still getting people to invest, so we would take people out sailing and he would dazzle them by flying a hull. *Mickey Muñoz*

BOTTOM: This shot was taken from the top of the crane that we used to lift the boats out of the water every day. The soft-rig boat we could set in its cradle, but because the sail was always up on the hard-rig boat, we had to set on its side so the sail was horizontal to the ground. That's me on the left, 2nd from the top. *Mickey Muñoz Collection*

OPPOSITE PAGE: The hard-rig version sailing. *Mickey Muñoz*

The Materials Evolution– Design Evolution Connection

Polyester resin, close tolerance urethane foam blanks, and the attitude "if it ain't broke why fix it" stagnated the progression of surfing for years. The evolution started again around the time Clark foam went out of business.

That Clark foam went out of business was one of the best things to happen to surfing. Clark was so good at what he did he had very little competition. He supplied the industry with high-quality foam blanks at a reasonable price with great customer service for years. Shapers could get blanks that replicated their designs. It made shaping more efficient and gave the shapers a benchmark for tracking design changes when they made them. Between the blanks and the use of polyester resin, that was relatively inexpensive and easy to use, the surfboard business could supply the growing demand, and it hummed along, status quo, for years.

Building surfboards has never been a high-profit business, so the motivation for change, other than how to make more profit, was generally not there. Businesses that had become complacent and depended on Clark Foam for their blanks were left scrambling when Clark shut his doors and went out of business without warning. Clark made sure that all his long-term and loyal customers got first pick of what inventory was left, but when the dust cleared and all the blanks were gone, many manufacturers were left with board orders they couldn't fill.

Even the existing foam manufacturers couldn't supply enough foam. The door was open for new entrepreneurs to jump into the business to try and fill the demand. Some of them came up with pretty good foam, but they didn't have the same blank designs or the variety that Clark had nor the accuracy in gluing the blanks. Trying to shape blanks that were not designed for your production models and that are not accurately glued slowed production and made replicating models difficult and sometimes impossible to do.

It was time for change. Clark Foam going out of business forced the surfboard industry to look at other types of foam and construction. Polyurethane foam can be glassed with either polyester or epoxy resin, but EPS (expanded polystyrene) foam, which is readily available, has to be glassed using epoxy resin. Most of the industry had been reluctant to use epoxy even though it's a much stronger resin than polyester resin, because epoxy is more expensive, it requires different techniques in application, takes more time to cure, and there are some misunderstandings about its toxicity.

EPS foam comes in large blocks like loaves of bread; you need to cut it to the length and width of the board, and thick enough to shape in the rocker. The different foam system and having to use epoxy resin forces new problem solving and thinking. It's a lot to ask of an industry that has used a set system successfully for more than forty years.

The pluses and minuses of any change could be discussed at length, but I think the "surging" scenario applies. You can continue, head down, in the main stream with little chance of getting out, or you can ride the countercurrents that change your perspective.

I think the industry right now is in the countercurrent; there is lots of experimenting going on in equipment design, manufacturing, and surfing. Each of the mainstay production methods has strengths and weaknesses: custom polyester, molded, and EPS/epoxy boards all have their place.

Surfers are pushing the boundaries beyond what was thought possible a few years ago; all of it combined is what fires evolution and stoke. Take the exploration of the finless *alaia* boards – perhaps the first surfboards that surfers ever stood on. Made from wood and finished with oil, you could shape one with fire and rocks. Surfers today are blowing minds with the lines they can carve on these boards.

There are so many little subtleties that go into design that make it stimulating and never totally resolved. The shaping and the designing end of it is part of a circle. That's why I've never lost my fascination for design and, consequently, my fascination for surfing.

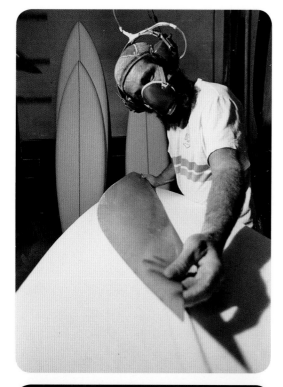

TOP:
The circle of shaping. *Art Brewer*

BOTTOM:
We shaped all kinds of boards in the early '70s. *Mickey Muñoz Collection*

OPPOSITE PAGE:
Shaping an early windsurfer. *Mickey Muñoz Collection*

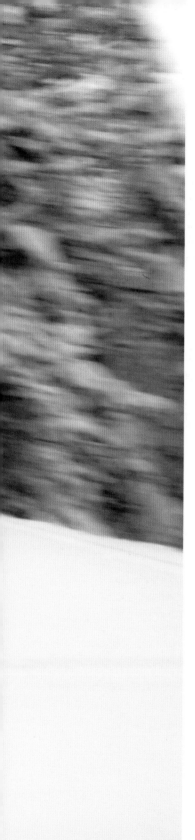

Snowboarding

I had been skiing since the '50s, and when the early snowboards came out, I tried one, but the gear wasn't really dialed yet. A couple years later, when the equipment got better, Peggy and I were up at Tahoe and decided to take a snowboard lesson, and from that time on, I never looked back. I never got on skis again after that first lesson.

Peggy's brother, John, bought a house in Mammoth and a brand new pair of skis. He got into snowboarding, and that was it for the skis. With his house up there and season passes, it made it reasonably affordable to go snowboarding. So we really got into it.

A couple of years into it, I was a better snowboarder than I ever was as a skier. There are a lot of similarities between surfing and snowboarding. Snow is slow moving water, the mountain is a wave, and you're in a surf stance: You are surfing.

Snowboarding was fun, but I also got interested in the design and construction of the equipment. When snowboarding was growing exponentially, a friend from Japan called me and asked if I knew any snowboard manufacturers that could build 2,500 to 3,000 boards. He had the orders and needed them as soon as possible. The SIA (Ski Industry Association) trade show in Las Vegas was just about to open; it's the biggest retail snow show in the United States, and I knew all players would be there.

They were there and laughing, "We can put you on a list, and maybe we'll get to you in two or three years." they replied to my inquiries. But while I was there I ran into a couple of surfers who were making snowboard cores out of wood. I asked them if they could glue some up with light and dark colored stringers, maybe add nose and tail blocks, and clear glass them; we would have something different from the rest of the pack. A couple of weeks later, we were in the snowboard business.

Well sort of: There were problems, problems that would take a lot more money than any of us had to invest. A year into it and we were just about "belly up." I walked through the next SIA tradeshow with one of our boards in hand and a guy approached me, and asked if I would be interested in talking with his company. It turned out he was from Santa Monica canyon, I knew his dad and we had a bunch of mutual friends. His company was making wooden snowboards, and he believed there was a big crossover market between surfing and snowboarding. He asked if I would be interested in doing a signature snowboard model with them. Timing is everything.

Arbor Snowboards, his company, had solved a lot of the problems we had run into. Their boards were beautiful and functional. The Arbor guys were smart, hardworking, and passionate about their business and life in general. It is still a good ride even though they no longer produce my model, they are still in business, going strong, and we are still friends, and we are still snowboarding.

We had hiked into the backcountry; I was with Yvon and two other free heelers. Thank goodness they were kind enough to wait for me. On the ascents, I was on snowshoes while they were on skis: big difference. Teton Pass. *Angus Thuermer*

Sailing
and Surfing

I've had some great adventures on some of the most efficient and radical sailing boats out there. Luck again got me right in on the leading edge of that.

Today, people are sailing around the world faster than any power vessel has; that's a huge accomplishment! A testament to the engineering and human stamina involved. To be at that high a level for that long a period of time and to pull it off is amazing. It's like stepping onto the moon.

There are a lot of parallels between contemporary surfing, towing, slab riding, and transocean sailing. The principles in the head and in what it takes to do it are similar. You just don't go out there on an 80-foot boat and throw yourself into 100-foot wave and pull that off.

I know they're riding huge waves towing in. They're riding slabs that make me want to throw up. Surfing in the last 10 years has developed to an incredible level, but aspiring to a 100-foot wave in midocean with no helicopter or Jet Ski around to save you and no mommy to call is an entirely unique experience. You're riding an 80-foot surfboard, a self-propelled surfboard, and you're towing yourself into these big ocean waves.

Surfing is fairly simple: It only has a few elements. These high-tech sailboats have more elements involved to make it possible to do what they do – to ride a 100-foot wave on a big boat

like that. It's the human element that connects sailing and surfing and the human element that keeps those big boats together.

There is so much more to it than just steering the boat. You have to constantly walk around on those boats with a tool apron on and tighten bolts; you've got to keep it all together. The loads are phenomenal.

I had a great sailing and surfing experience on *Double Bullet* in one of the Transpac races. *Double Bullet* was a big catamaran around 75 feet long that had no cabin, but the hulls were big enough to sleep in. *Bullet* was cold-molded – a really beautiful boat, beautiful hulls – but the rig, with its 100-foot mast and huge winches, left a lot to be desired. It was probably the most dangerous boat I'd ever sailed on because of the rig. It had these death triangles where if a fitting gave way, you're in the middle

of a crossbow. *Cur-rack!* something breaks, and you might get a shackle imbedded in your head at a zillion miles an hour.

I think it was 35 feet wide; you could imagine when flying a hull with that wide a boat that the loading on the rig was just unbelievable. This is a big boat, big gear, and fast. At 20 knots, you're thinking, "Is something dragging? Have we got kelp on the rudders, what's going on?" When you hit 30 knots, you're thinking, "Oh, OK, now we're finally moving. This boat was easily capable of breaking the existing record and setting a new one.

On the afternoon of day four of the race, we came upon a line squall that looked like a big-walled, point-wave at Rincon: an endless black and gray line that was 400 or 500 feet high. It was this huge wave. At the same time, we had this big ocean swell behind us and just the right wind velocity. We felt like we

were on a 75-foot surfboard, and we were riding this line squall.

Usually, you sail by feeling the subtle changes in wind direction and velocity – but this one you could see; it was a visual wave. We knew where we were in relation to it, and we rode it like we were on a surfboard: off the bottom up into the wave, then release, driving off the wave, and gaining speed. As the apparent wind builds up and moves forward, you can trim around the sections and get in the barrel. It's surfing at a very high level, and it lasted for hours.

ABOVE:
Malia at speed. *Mickey Muñoz*

OPPOSITE PAGE:
These guys look to be having a fun time in the Ala Moana channel. *Jamie Ballenger*

Wind Warrior

Wind Warrior was an open 48-foot coastal racing catamaran that Steve Schidler, the owner, decided he wanted to race to Hawai'i. It was a Spartan race boat, so a few weeks before the race we built this little 18-inch high shelter on the trampoline. It was so small that the big guys in the crew had to crawl back outside to turn over, but it did keep our gear dry and provided a shelter to crawl into out of the wind and rest in a sleeping bag. The boat was light; it had a trampoline and a rotating rig.

The first night out from Long Beach, we were out beyond San Nicholas Island at about 11:00. The wind was blowing about 30 knots, and we were hauling ass through big swells, gnarly seas, cold water, and pitch-black. It gets shitty out there in that stretch of water: You get all the spin off of Points Arguello and Conception. The wind accelerates as it goes out across San Miguel Island toward San Nicholas Island where there's nothing that grows any higher than a foot or two.

All of a sudden we heard a *Cur-rack!* We had broken one of the two daggerboards. I was the unlucky one who got to strip off all my clothes, tie a line around my waist, and with a flashlight in my hand go under the boat to get this broken daggerboard that was flopping back and forth, still attached by fiberglass. My job was to cut this board away and get it onboard so we could get sailing again.

That was spooky; I felt like bait. We finally got that all together, and I got back on board and got warm. It was a pretty gnarly start for a sailing race to Hawai'i.

The second day out, we broke a rudder, which left us with only one rudder and one daggerboard. Then on the third day out, we lost all our electronics. They were kept in the captain's domain, a little space inside one of the hulls that was maybe 3 feet wide by 5 feet high. He kept it closed up for warmth, and condensation built up, killing the radio and the electrical instruments. We were left with nothing but a handheld VHF radio, a compass, and a sextant. So we did what the hippies did – follow the contrails – and haul ass.

Prior to hitting the trades, it had been cold and overcast, but now in the trades, the cloud layer broke up, and the scattering big puffy clouds revealed the moon. I was on watch with another guy, and we were in this zone where the waves were getting behind us and building into these large pyramids.

It was probably one of the most ethereal sailing adventures I've ever had. I refused to get off the helm – it was surfing at its best. We never went under 20 knots, ever, and we were up in the 30-plus bracket a lot. For a little boat, close to the water, that's hauling ass.

And we were riding waves, good-sized waves where you could stuff a bow into the backside of the wave ahead and really mess up. But it was a really consistent wind, and we had up what we called the "fly's wing," a big, beautiful translucent reaching sail. It shimmered in the moonlight, the ocean glowed with bioluminescence, there were big ocean swells, and the wind direction was perfect. We followed the silver path of the moon through the waves; it was the only light around.

Racing to Hawai'i, alone in the middle of the ocean, a thousand miles from anywhere, and we were frickin' surfing.

CLOCKWISE FROM TOP:
Accommodations were virtually nonexistent, and we ate a lot of PB&Js on that trip. *Mickey Muñoz*

The view out of the "igloo" gives you a perspective on how small it was. *Mickey Muñoz*

The fly's wing. *Mickey Muñoz*

Speed
and Control

Before I actually started shaping surfboards in production, I worked for Carter Pyle building monohulls and catamarans. Catamarans were among the highest performance boats at that time. There were some planing monohull boats that held world speed records, primarily scows. The International Finn, a 14-foot closely monitored class boat with an unsupported rotating mast – that we actually manufactured – had the second-fastest official speed of any sailboat in the world at that time.

Catamarans came along, and they consistently sailed faster than monohulls. It was because of the stability of the catamaran. They could have more sail area – and be able to control the forces from that sail area – because their hulls were spread apart and therefore provided tremendous stability. The International Finn depended on the solo sailor as moveable ballast to keep the boat flat, the scow depended on some keel ballast and moveable crew to counter the force of the sails and keep them flat and planing. They both took a great deal of skill to sail. Their speed was limited by the amount of power and how you control it. Theoretically, the planing hulls have little limit in their top-end speed and someday may exceed that of the displacement multihulls, but the future right now is in foils both in the water and out. Creating power and lift while reducing drag – controlling the forces is what its all about.

The catamaran allowed you to control the speed better because of the stability due to the width of the boat. You had the leverage of the wide hulls, where a little moveable crew weight on the rail was enough to hold them flat.

I learned a lot about airfoils and underwater foils working on those boats. I learned about water displacement – displacement hulls as opposed to planing hulls. And I tried to translate some of those ideas into surfboard designs.

In surfboard design, the way riders were able to control the speed from *paipo* boards was that they were prone and holding on; if average surfers of the time tried standing on those boards, they probably couldn't have surfed them in those big Waimea waves. It was the same with Greenough's kneeboards. The *paipo* riders would take advantage of the big drop to generate a huge amount speed as they went down the wave and shot along the bottom at many times the speed of anything around them. When they finally slowed down enough, they could turn the board back into the wave and maintain. George sacrificed a little of that all-out speed for control; that's why he was able to pull off these carving S-turns – planing S-turns at speed.

How to create speed and control speed, how to create lift and control lift are pretty thought-provoking concepts. By swinging the design pendulum out in one extreme direction, you learn how to create certain performance features – like lift or speed. However, the outer swing of that pendulum is so specialized that if you want more all-around performance or to really control whatever attributes you have created, then the pendulum needs to come back toward the middle again.

CLOCKWISE FROM LEFT:
10,000 feet and glassy. *Mickey Muñoz Collection*

Lift and controlling lift. *Mickey Muñoz Collection*

Waimea Bay. *Peter French*

Bodysurfing at the Wedge. *Bud Browne*

Paddleboard Design

I made some 12-foot rescue paddleboards for the lifeguards. I was testing the first one I made in Dana Point harbor soon after I made it. Craig Lockwood was also designing and building a 12-foot paddleboard that he called the Waterman, and he just happened to be testing his at the same location and launched within minutes of me.

The boards were the same length, but they were almost the reverse of each other. You could almost put the fin on the nose of mine and get his board, and vice versa. Mine had a fine entry and a wide, square tail; his had a rounded entry and a fine tail. We were both about the same size and the same ability, so we paddled together around the island in the Dana Point harbor. At the end, we were pretty darn even. I don't remember who beat who to the sand, but we were within 10 feet of each other.

We traded boards and did the same thing and got the same results. We never paddled outside the harbor in the bump to see what the differences were in rough water, but on flat water, the speed of the two boards was nearly identical. I have always wondered about that: Is it the entry or the exit?

I outfitted my last truck with a custom Callen Camper, and I was worried about the frontal area and wanted to redesign the curves. I didn't, but only after I conferred with my friend Richard Tracey. Richard said don't worry about the front, the back is where most of the drag is. When you look at one of those 1950s teardrop trailers, they had it right for reducing drag. They weren't so practical for living, but they were right for reducing drag.

So Craig may have had it right, but the designs sure seemed even when we tested them side-by-side that day in Dana.

ABOVE:
Early paddleboard design: On the left is Craig Lockwood's Waterman shape. *Mickey Muñoz*

OPPOSITE PAGE: From an ad photo shoot: On the left, Phil Edwards and I are holding the paddleboard I shaped; note the fine bow and wide tail. On the right, Hobie Alter and his son Jeff show off a Hobie shape. Poche. *Art Brewer*

This is a model trimaran I made for Randy Smyth, a sailmaker and world-class multihull sailor. I traded him the model for a sail.
Mickey Muñoz

Design to Suit the Need

Every body is different, surfing styles are different, every surf break is different; those differences influence design.

Let's take boats as an example. For me the perfect boat would be a seaworthy, fast, efficient, motor-sailing catamaran. It would not only sail fast but would be capable of powering as fast as it could sail. It would be small enough and uncomplicated enough to be operated by one person, but big enough to carry the toys and have the amenities to make it comfortable to live on.

Once I get where I'm going, I want to be able to anchor the boat, live on it, and use it as a platform for the stuff I enjoy: being in the water, diving, fishing, exploring islands   I want to surf, and I want to explore the world. That's one vehicle and one way I approach my design parameters; suit the need.

Whatever it is – designing boats, surfboards, skis, clothes, cars – it's that kind of juggling of criteria that you're doing. If you only drive from your home to your office, then you design a vehicle that is super economical. You don't need a huge amount of cargo space; you need to carry your briefcase and one other passenger. I'm a surfer, and I need – or I perceive I need – a vehicle where I can keep my equipment, wetsuits, boards, fins, paddles, repair stuff, tools, camp gear, and a bed. It all comes back to your needs or perceived needs.

My perceived needs in boats have evolved over the years after I sold *Malia*. Our next boat was a little English design called a Hirondelle, a 23-foot catamaran made for sailing rough water around Britain. Look at a well-designed old surfboard, airplane, or boat, and for the most part, the '50s lines are as valid as the newer ones. It doesn't matter when they were designed; a line that is a classic line, will be a classic line a thousand years from now. Styles will change, and the way you use that line will change, but those lines are going to be around forever. Having been around boats most of my life, I looked at that '50s-era English boat, and it looked seaworthy – a classic design that could be reshaped into a perfect surf vehicle.

I remodeled it to be a boat for diving, surfing, and hanging out near surf breaks. If I ever got caught in a situation where I had to put the boat on the beach, either running it straight in or riding a wave in, this boat could do it.

Peggy's a teacher and only gets so much time off. The island we like to go to is 55 miles away; to sail there is an all-day affair unless you get some magic wind or you're on an incredibly fast boat. The problem with a fast-sailing catamaran is they aren't good load carriers; to be efficient, they have to be light . . . or big. For us to go to the islands with our toys, we needed to be able to power. I mucked around with different concepts for the rig, but as much as I like sailing, I like being at the islands more, so I took the mast off, which reduced pitching, weight, and windage, and put twin outboards on it. I put a hard-top on it with a surfboard and kayak rack. With twin Hondas, it was economical to run. Its displacement hull limited its top-end speed, but for real-world messing around in the ocean it was plenty fast enough, and it had a lot of rocker, which let me surf the boat.

I lengthened the boat a couple feet, adding to each transom, and fashioned a "tailgate" off the trailing edge of the wingdeck, which was hinged so you could let it down in the water. This allowed our water dogs to be able to swim up and on to the platform and get up to the bridge deck on their own. I got tired of lifting wet 60- to 80-pound dogs out of the water. It made them totally independent. It turned out that was a really good for every other water activity from cleaning fish to washing dishes to

Gino Morrelli and Randy inspect an earlier stage of the same model. *Mickey Muñoz*

diving, fishing, surfing and just about anything you'd need and want as a water person – that tailgate made the boat.

The hulls were displacement hulls as opposed to planing hulls. Planing is very efficient after you get to the point where you're planing. You have to have enough surface area to plane, and it takes a lot of horsepower to get up on a plane. Displacing is not as fast, but it can be very efficient. In my mind, the real world of boating is not planing across the ocean. I don't need to get there that fast; I just want to be able to beat the weather, go at an efficient speed, and get there in a reasonable amount of time. You get to see and feel what's around you on the journey.

We had a lot of fun with that boat. It had a little bit of a down-stairs cabin so you could get out of the weather. Peggy and I took it all over the Channel Islands and to places where you've got to have your act together. It could have gone anywhere, far north or far south . . . but like any smart boater, before we even sold her, we bought a bigger boat.

Our next boat was a larger catamaran that had been slipped in front of our boat for 10 years and had hardly been used. A divorce forced the owners to sell. It was an OK deal, and it was just too easy to do. The design was a blowup of the boat we had – instead of 23 feet long, it was 32 feet.

I've done some work on it, but was hampered by uncertainties in the harbor plan. And then stand-up surfing came along, and I really got involved in that – in designing and participating. That took my design and creative energy away from the boat.

I'll leave the rig up for now, but eventually I want to take the rig off for the same reasons I took it off the little boat. I still want to work on efficiency, and I would like to go back to the concept of motor sailing, but now I'm thinking of doing it with a kite. I think I could have the best of both worlds with kites. They've got kites now that are very efficient – small and light, perfect for launching from the deck of a catamaran. There's a company that makes kites to assist freighters: In the right conditions, they're able to fly kites and save fuel.

Nature's Engineering: Think Like a Rock

Nature is probably the best designer of all; it always suits the need. Stuff in nature has been around a long time and has figured out how to endure, how to survive. The designs evolve over time and make sense.

Look at the bones of pelicans. Birds have to have light but strong bones; they've got to be able to fly. When you look at those bones, they give you a hint at how the tendons and muscles attach to them to cantilever the wings out and spread the load. You can take that and apply it to design in boats and surfboards. Multihulls have two hulls cantilevered a certain distance apart. There's a lot of engineering that goes into keeping those hulls from breaking off and keeping the rig up. You can get design clues on how to structure that from looking at nature.

I'm also fascinated by the aesthetics. It's the visual stuff that turns me on and keeps me stimulated. You can see it in the composition, the color, and the shape of natural items. Rocks are fascinating to me; in my mind, rocks are just very slow moving water. They're changing shape and composition all the time. It's just happening over a long, long period of time.

We have a place in Baja on the side of an arroyo, and nothing is level. It doesn't rain much down there, but when it rains, it really rains. Every rock, every ledge, every little irregularity in the ground has a drainage, a way that the water drains off; otherwise, everything ends up in the ocean. We quarry those rocks to use for building. Peggy and I are not very big, so we have had to trick rocks into getting in our truck and going where we want them to go.

One of the first tools that I invested in down there was a pinch bar. It is about a 7-foot long steel bar; with leverage you can do big things. Between that and a lot of engineering trickery, we have moved some huge rocks weighing in the hundreds of pounds. If you get in a hurry and get impatient, you get hurt. The rock tips over and crushes your foot or your hand or breaks your pinch bar or hurts you in some other way – badly. So you have to think like a rock. You have to slow down, and you have to think what that rock would do, how that rock would move – and how to move it.

Peggy and I have built rock retaining walls and backfilled them with smaller and smaller rocks, down to the size of arroyo sand; in some places, we use pavers and set those in the sand. They have all withstood some pretty horrendous rains; walls built to hold back the rain are the ones that get in trouble. We put our walls up without mortar, so they're really like filters.

It's very fun to play with the rocks and learn to nest and fit them into one another. Once you figure that out, once you see how they physically get to where they are, then you know how to undo them. When we quarry a 400- or 500-pound rock, we manage to get that rock out of the ground and up into our truck. I think we learned how the pyramids were built.

One of my few regrets in life is not meeting Yvon Chouinard 50 years before I did and being able to hang out in Yosemite and climb with him. I think I would have loved climbing. I love the engineering: I think those guys had to think like rocks.

ABOVE:
Casa de Muñoz, Cabo. *Mickey Muñoz*

OPPOSITE PAGE:
The beach in front of our place in Cabo.
Mickey Muñoz

Sea Lion Attack

Peggy and I sailed to Santa Barbara Island with a mutual girlfriend of ours named Patty. Santa Barbara Island is a little island. It's a rock. It's about a mile and a quarter across and a half-mile wide. I've paddled around the whole island in a couple of hours; you could swim around it, but I wouldn't; it's whitie territory. It's like a lazy Susan for great white sharks, a smorgasbord: everything from California sea lions, to northern fur seals, to harbor seals, to elephant seals. And there are thousands and thousands and thousands of seals and sea lions.

On the first day there, we anchored around the back side in a little cove. I rigged up my gear to go dive and get our dinner. Peggy and Patty were just going to hang out on deck. I jumped over the side and went down to 45 feet. The kelp forest was thick and close together. I'm always uncomfortable on the first dive of a trip, it takes me a while to sort out and adjust my gear, but I managed to spear a good-sized calico, and as I was pulling in the fish, it wove its way through the kelp. I juggled my gun while pulling in the shooting line, got the fish, pulled it off the spear and put it on the string. A sea lion dove on me to check me out and was really interested in my fish.

I've given sea lions fish before, and normally they won't eat the fish; they just end up playing with it. So this time I figured I wasn't going to give away my fish. The sea lion got pissed off, and I could see the look in its eyes. It got increasingly aggressive. I turned my gun around and used the butt of the gun to fend off the sea lion. I was at a loss for what else to do. I still had my shooting line wrapped around some kelp, and I was trying to get my act together while trying to fend off this sea lion that was bigger than me.

There's a reason they're called sea lions: They're not shy, and they have sharp teeth. I was starting to get really worried, and my adrenaline kicked in. I wanted to know where the boat was and how far I had to go to get to it. I knew better, but I just kicked straight up to get to the surface. In thick kelp that isn't a good idea.

I broke through the kelp and surfaced. I was jamming the butt of my spear gun down at the sea lion as it came up behind me, biting my fins the whole way up. I pulled my mouthpiece out and looked around for the boat. The kelp was wrapped around my tank and the rebound started to drag me back under. I was still hitting the sea lion with my gun, trying to fend it off. I lost my regulator and mouthpiece, and I was starting to hyperventilate. I saw the boat. Peggy looked over at me and I yelled to her; I was at the panic point.

I got one breath before I was dragged under and I was starting to run out of air. I tried to find my mouthpiece, while still fending off the sea lion. A voice in my head finally clicked in and told me I better relax or I was going to drown then and there. I had to think of it just like a big wave, I had to discipline myself to not fight it. So I did just that, and I surged back up and got a little bit of air, and then found my mouthpiece again. I flipped over on my back and thought to myself, "OK, if I get bitten, I get bitten; that's what I have to deal with. I have to breathe before I worry about that."

Meanwhile, without hesitation, Peggy got up and dove off the boat and swam for me, and she is a fast swimmer. She got to me and helped me untangle the kelp, and we worked our way back to the boat. We got to the side of the boat; she got out, and I handed her my gear. Meanwhile, I was still getting attacked by the sea lion and was still retaliating with the butt of my gun.

Finally, I got all my shit off, got on the boat deck, and just lay there recovering. I looked over the side, and the sea lion was still there looking right at me. I took my fin and slammed it down in the water next to the sea lion, thinking I would scare it away. Instead it just curled its lips back and snarled at me. The sea lion stayed there until we got the motor started and pulled the anchor. It followed us out of the cove, and it wasn't until we rounded the corner that it turned and left.

The next day, we went to the main cove where there is a landing. We went for a hike and passed the ranger station. The ranger was there, and I asked him if he ever heard of anyone getting attacked by a sea lion out at the island.

"That was you?" he exclaimed. "I wasn't sure what it was at first. I thought it could be a shark attack." He had seen my whole ordeal from land. "Glad you made it; the paperwork would have been horrible."

You don't want to tangle with this guy in the water. *Mickey Muñoz*

Handling Crowds

When I first started surfing, there were more waves than surfers. Malibu would get crowded once in a while, but not that crowded, not compared to like it is today, where there are more surfers than waves in the best spots. The way I look at it, the crowds are a catalyst for creativity. As surfing has become more popular, even the beachbreaks and the more esoteric breaks are now crowded with surfers. It has forced surfers to explore other options: boat access breaks, distant travel to exotic locations. The crowds force you to seek waves in places that most people can't get to. That was one of my main motivating factors to get involved in boats and boat design.

One way to deal with crowds is to invent games that keep you moving in the lineup. We used to play the game of travel surfing – as opposed to surf travel – that I played just recently. We used to park at San Onofre and surf at Lower Trestles. The goal was to surf your way back to the parking lot at San Onofre. The loose rules were that you couldn't paddle toward the destination except in the case of avoiding a collision or avoiding getting pounded. The rules are only suggestions because you can play it any way you want. It was OK to paddle a little in the direction of travel in order to catch a wave, but you didn't want to just paddle straight to the mark; you wanted to try to surf your way there.

By adhering to the rules, you could learn a lot. You learned about surfing, about the fact that there are no bad waves, and about riding the wave behind the wave. You also learned about riding close out beachbreaks. You learned about going right on left-breaking waves.

The surf was really good the other day, and I ended up at Church and played the game back to the lot. I pulled out over the top of my last wave and was still gliding down coast, which is legal because I wasn't paddling. I got into the shorebreak area – it's a nasty shorebreak. You can get hurt there. It was just before dark, and the sun had been down for a half an hour. There were two girls still on the beach; they were 30 feet from me. A little wedge came along, a right-hander that would take me toward the parking lot. It was in the beachbreak zone, so it was a pretty critical wave.

I took off and was locked in and riding in two feet of water on a waist-high wave. Coming the other direction right into the curl and absolutely in trim was a full-grown male sea lion, a 400- to 500-pounder. He took off on the shoulder, and I never saw him. He didn't see me until we were five feet apart on a collision course. I heard the girls on the beach scream as they watched this impending crash. I don't know how that sea lion made it under me, but he did. I thought I was going to put a fin gash down his back and I would end up in the water in a fight with a really, big dude. I didn't hit the sea lion. I rode another 20 feet, pulled out, and stepped off into a foot of water.

There are still plenty of waves to ride; the crowds just force you farther and farther out. That's the wonderful hook about surfing: It's always changing and it's always challenging. The latest evolution of stand-up surfing has allowed us to ride waves that you wouldn't normally ride on a conventional board. It's opened up a whole new area of surfing, as well as fitness – along with the sheer pleasure of being in the water.

The crowds are also spurring a lot of innovation in surfboard design. It reminds me of the progression in the early days when new surfers got pushed out into the beachbreaks, and that resulted in boards being shaped for beachbreak conditions. With Clark Foam going out of business and the influence of the thruster-style board no longer so strong, other designs are being explored. I was at Noosa recently, and Tom Wegener had made a 16-foot, 250-pound *olo* board. I heard the guy that rode it, rode the heck out of it.

There is a whole group of kids riding basically the same shapes that we were riding in the '60s, and they are riding them like we never did. They're hanging 10 in waves that there's no way I could have ever done, and I was a pretty good noserider.

ABOVE: One of our original reasons to get into boating was to get away from the crowds, even back then. *Mickey Muñoz*

OPPOSITE PAGE: On board *Swallow Swift*, our heavily modified Hirondelle. *Jeff Divine*

Bill Wise

I met Bill Wise when I was working for Hobie Alter. I would go back to the East Coast to service the dealers in the summer. I would fly to Miami, rent a car, and work my way up the coast to Maine. I went to the dealers along the way and schmoozed, talked board designs, and made sure they had all the right stuff.

Bill Wise was a dealer in Maryland. Bill was a family man and a real water guy: diver, surfer, former lifeguard. He took me surfing on a funky blown-out, knee-high day in Maryland. We had been out there for a while when Bill took off on a wave. I turned to look inside for him, and I didn't see Bill, only his board floating upside down. I looked harder and spotted him on the inside, face down in the water. I paddled in, got to him, and lifted his head out of the water. He was fully conscious but drowning in 3 feet of water. I slid him onto my board and yelled for help because Bill was a pretty big guy. A kid on the beach helped me get him to the beach and then called an ambulance. Bottom line: He broke his neck and became a quadriplegic.

He went through a tough time after that. He once told me, "There were times I wish you hadn't saved me. I would have given up. I would have just as soon not gone through this."

A full day for him would be to get up, take a dump, eat breakfast, brush his teeth, and then get back in bed.

Bill persevered though. He learned to write with a pencil in his mouth. He learned to shoot photos with his camera; he would use his tongue to set up his camera and shoot pictures. And Bill never stopped surfing; he surfed vicariously. He still loved surfing.

People would send him talismans from all over the world. I sent him a pelican feather from San Clemente Island; others would send him rocks or shells or whatever it was they found at their favorite surf spots. He hung the talismans above his bed, and he would vicariously fly on the feather or visit the beach with the shell. People would take him to the ocean where he could watch surfing and take pictures; he also wrote about surfing.

His wife Rosalie and their kids stuck with him the whole time. It wasn't easy; Bill couldn't work, and they didn't have any money.

Dick Matts and Hobie were both his good friends, and they both helped him over the years. We stayed in touch; at first, it was letters, cards, and the telephone. When the computer came along, he got a voice recognition program, and then he started to write prolifically. He started to communicate all over the world. Bill had run the gamut of emotion and physical disabilities and had conquered a lot of it. Bill became a mentor for a lot of people around the world. He was truly an amazing guy.

Almost 25 years from the date that he broke his neck, Hobie and Dick brought Bill out here to hang out with us and visit his old friends. I had planned a surprise for him when he came out: I was going to take him surfing. I told him he should come out on our boat. He said he would really like to do that, along with his wife, Rosalie, who had been on a boat once in her life.

He got out here, and after three or four days of partying, he was pretty tired; it was a big deal for him to do that level of activity. He started to waver on the boat trip, but I convinced him that he should come. On the day of the boat trip, I rigged up a piece of plywood as a ramp, and we rolled his wheelchair onto the boat and strapped him in behind the front fairing so he could see but was protected from the spray.

It was springtime and the weather was a little funky, but it was the nicest day of the week. We took off from Dana Point with Bill, his wife, Peggy, me, and another friend, Richard Brassard. We sailed down the coast toward Trestles on a head-high day. We got to Cottons, and Bill was stoked to see surfing from the perspective of a boat. We went farther down to Upper Trestles, and Bill was getting more and more stoked, as was Rosalie.

We got to Lowers right as a set came in, so I took off on a wave with the boat. There was Bill, strapped into a 32-foot catamaran and surfing again. It was quite a surprise. There were a couple people riding behind us on the wave and they were hooting; we

were hooting. Bill tried to do a Quasimodo in his wheel chair, and Rosalie was in shock. It was the second time she had ever been on a boat, and she was surfing.

We pulled out of the wave, and both Bill and I were in tears. He never thought he would ride a wave again – ever. The last time we surfed together, he broke his neck. It was a pretty big commitment for both of us. We pulled out of the wave and glided out into the flats; the surfers were cheering, and he was just beside himself.

We ended up anchoring, and Peggy, Richard, and I went surfing. We came back to the boat as the sun was setting, and Rosalie was sitting in Bill's lap – it was a beautiful sunset and very romantic for them.

That experience inspired Bill and Rosalie to take scuba lessons. Imagine being a quadriplegic under water; it must be like being in space. Suddenly that labor of moving 200 pounds around is gone. They sent us a picture of the two of them with their mouthpieces out kissing underwater.

When anybody asks me what the best wave I've ever ridden, that ride with Bill is probably it.

CLOCKWISE FROM TOP LEFT:
Bill Wise and I hugging after we rode the wave on *Malia*. *Mickey Muñoz Collection*

The *Quasimodo*. *Mickey Muñoz*

Bill's first wave in a long time. *Mickey Muñoz*

From left to right: Rosalie Wise, Bill, Richard Brassard, and Peggy Muñoz. *Mickey Muñoz*

131

The *Quasimodo*

The *Quasimodo* was just me goofing around. The actual shot comes from a frame grab off a 16 mm film that John Severson shot in the late '50s at Arroyo Secos after Rincon had blown out. The conditions are often slightly offshore there when other places blow out, so if Bobby Patterson and I needed to surf some more on our way back down the coast, which we always did, we would go out there.

Our usual routine was to drive up the coast and surf Overhead if the conditions were right. We had a ritual at Overhead: One of us would paddle on one side of the peak, and the other would paddle on the other side. The idea was to wait for a set and each be in such a position that we could look through the tube at each other. When Overhead blew out, we would go to Rincon and ride there. After that we would come back and ride Secos on the way back in the evening.

One particular day, Bobby and I were driving down from Rincon where we had been riding all morning, and Severson was about a half an hour behind us. Bobby and I went out at Secos, and John saw our car there and stopped to shoot some film.

In those days, we were enamored with bull fighting and went to see the bull fights in Tijuana a lot. There was a lot of flowery stuff done in bull fighting – a lot of moves that were very dangerous and showy, and they had various names for them. We rode Malibu a lot, and because it was such a perfect wave, we had endless hours to entertain each other by doing different poses and maneuvers inspired by bull fighting. We had the *mysterioso*, the *el spontáneo*, the *el telephono*, and others – all just stupid, spontaneous moves that made us laugh. We didn't really think much about it at the time; it was just a thing we did. That's what we were doing that day at Secos.

A couple of weeks later, I was with John, and he went over the film in his moviola, which was a hand crank affair where you rolled the film through a little window and could look at it frame by frame. We came to this particular wave and John stopped the film because we both liked the pose. We rolled the film back and forth until we settled on one image. At the time, we

The *Quasimodo*. *John Severson*

El Spontáneo. John Severson

were naming these stances and poses, and we came up with the name *Quasimodo*, because it sort of looked like the Hunchback of Notre Dame. I didn't think much about it, but John decided to print it in black and white. That's why the image is kind of grainy and graphic; it was a blow up from 16 mm color film into black and white. When John published the first *Surfer* magazine, he ran that photo as a feature photo.

That image became kind of famous because it was graphic and grabbed people's imagination when they thought of surfing. Eventually, I got permission to use it as my logo.

Probably 50 years after John filmed the Flea and I at Secos I got a call from a talent agency that was looking for an older surfer to be in a bank commercial. They asked if I would come up for a talent call. I had done this before: There were people in

SAG who are professional surfer-actors, they show up, and usually you don't have a chance against them. I would spend two and a half hours driving each way up to the Valley only to be told, "Sorry, you're the wrong type." So I turned them down.

A couple of hours later, the agency called back and said they couldn't get anybody from my area to come up and that they didn't want an actor – they wanted somebody real. I told them if they wanted people from Orange County, they should come and do the test down here. I told them I could get some people together, and we could do it at San Onofre.

Two days later, they came down, and the husband of the gal who owned the agency did the film test of the group of surfers I had gathered. The next morning, I got a call saying they had pared it down to three people and that I was one of them. Could I come up for a second call in Hollywood. That was a shorter drive than the Valley, so I agreed and showed up at the appointed time on the appointed day.

The woman from the agency asked if I had ever surfed at Secos as that was where they were shooting the commercial. "Yes, as a matter of fact I have," and I brought out my little package of photos. "That's where that photo was taken," and I showed her Severson's shot, and I told her the story, which she loved.

The three of us who got called back were in the waiting room – one, my longtime friend. My turn came second, before my friend. I walked in, and behind a table were the client, the bank people, the director, and the producer. They asked me to stand on a line and introduce myself. Someone noticed a cut on my lip and asked how I got it. I told them I had got it from my mouthpiece while diving. The follow-up question was whether I was a diver and did I have any diving stories.

"Well, as a matter of fact I have a shark story I could tell you," I replied and started into the story of Frank Donahue and the shark adventure. I got three-quarters of the way into the story and they were in hysterics, laughing like crazy and hooting. I finished up the story, and they asked if I would mind taking my shirt off and turning around. I replied I didn't mind taking everything off. So I did as they asked, and then we were done.

I walked out into the lobby and my friend asked, "What the hell did you tell them?" Apparently they could hear the laughter in the waiting room.

"I don't know; I was just talking story," I replied. I left and drove home. That night I got a call, saying I was the one and could I drive back up the next day for wardrobe and then be on the set the day after. We went to Secos for the shoot, but the problem is you can't kick people out of the water for an ad shoot, so I was competing with the other surfers for waves. We shot in the water all morning, then beach stuff until late afternoon. The sun was going down fast and they needed more water shots. They had three cameras set up on the beach, and a water photographer out in the break.

By now the water was pretty crowded with the after-work crew, and it wasn't very consistent nor a great day for waves at Secos. I got three or four waves and wound up on the inside. The director yelled, "OK, we've only got time for one more. The sun's going down; you got time for one more."

So I started to scramble. I paddled back out, and as a set came, a guy blew it on the outside and I took off on the wave and thought, "What the hell? Why not?" So I did the *Quasimodo* and pulled it off. I should have been wiped out because it was

a closeout, but it wasn't. The tail of my board spun out, and I proned in. They were in hysterics on the beach. The entire film crew was genuflecting. So 50 years later, I did my second *Quasimodo* at Secos, and actually got paid for it.

TOP: *El Telephono*. *John Severson*

BOTTOM: I figured I was pretty safe bull fighting a tied-up cow. North Shore. *Mickey Muñoz Collection*

Surfing Is the Fountain of Youth

I went with Yvon Chouinard on a Patagonia boat trip from Bali to Sumbawa and Lombok. I rode Scar Reef – aptly named – a very radical, dangerous place at triple overhead. I managed to get the biggest barrel I've ever been in – a stand-up left barrel. The youngest guy on the trip – 40 years younger than me – was paddling out at the time and looking right into the barrel. He was just shocked. I came flying out and over the edge with a big shit-eating grin, hooting, and yelling, "I can quit surfing now."

After that, we surfed some baby breaks, waves you could go out and giggle and laugh and still get in a barrel or two. Then we went to surf Desert Point, a very tide-fickle wave; get there at the wrong tide and it's absolutely flat, but four or five hours later it's arguably the finest wave in the world.

We had motored all night in this 60-foot steel ketch to get there and rounded the end of the island about midnight to get to Desert Point. The trades were blowing, and we had the sails up and were on a reach – the perfect point of sail – and we had the powerful diesel engine running, with that combination the boat should travel at around 10 knots. It took us four and a half hours to go the last four miles because of the current.

The setup at Desert Point with a southern hemisphere swell and the right tide has waves that come wheeling around the point like spokes on a bicycle wheel straight into that 10-knot current. It's one of those waves like Hanalei that grows in size the farther down the line you get. You takeoff and start racing, as the wave grows, the water from the previous wave that had built up on the reef drains off and flows into the current, compounding its effect. You can hear it and see it. It's like being flushed down a giant drain; only instead of heading down you are flying parallel to the reef inside the vortex running for your life.

I took off on a set wave, and the barrel I was in was, as they say, big enough to drive a truck through. As it was pitching out over my head I suddenly saw something in the water right in my path, and thought, "Oh, shit, I'm gonna hit a turtle," but it turned out to be the tail of Yvon's broken board that he was dragging through the wave.

Yvon had broken his board a couple of waves before the wave I took off on. He was standing on the reef in knee-deep water with the back half of his board in his arms, watching me on this wave and not knowing what to do because it was shallow and radical. I was so close to him that all he could think of doing is diving under the wave, but he had to dive flat because it was really shallow. I didn't even see him. I avoided the tail of Yvon's board and went another 100 yards down the wave.

I'm usually pretty positive when I get in those situations; you have to be. But on this wave, I was thinking there's no way I could make this wave. I kept going because I couldn't do anything else. I ended up making the wave another 100 yards and finally managed to somehow get out through the top of the wave and survive intact. I came out of that wave with a shit-eating grin, totally elated - one of those grins that lasts a lifetime.

Einstein had a theory he called "motion time dilation." If you could fly off in a rocket and accelerate past the speed of light, the closer you got to the speed of light, the more time would appear to slow down. Theoretically, if you could exceed the speed of light, you could catch up with time, passing it and coming back younger than when you left. Well, at least I think he meant something like that.

The illusion of speed in the wave at Desert Point is so great, that in my mind I exceeded the speed of light and came out younger than when I took off on it. I believe that those sorts of experiences are so profound, that some of the electrical impulses in your brain change, and that is a catalyst that promotes changes in some of your body chemistry. I have no doubt that my mind thinks younger and my body responds younger each time those peak experiences occur.

CLOCKWISE FROM TOP:
The aptly named Scar Reef: Most of the locals were bandaged and limping. *Mickey Muñoz*

Desert Point. *Mickey Muñoz*

Scar Reef. *Mickey Muñoz*

Chasing Dora

Wes Brown, Bruce Brown's grandson, called me and asked me if he could interview me. He knew that Miki Dora and I had known each other over a long period of time; he wanted to tell me of his idea for a film that concerned Dora and wanted to know what I thought of it. So he came by, and the more we talked about the idea, the more interested in it I became. Finally, he asked if I would be interested in being part of the film. I immediately said yes.

The concept for the film was based on an article that Miki had written for *The Surfer's Journal* called "The Aquatic Ape" a fair time ago. His concept was for a contest where the surfers who participated would design and build their own boards out of strictly natural materials. The board could be any length but had to have a 10-inch square-tail and a single fin. The surfer also had to wear natural materials. There would be no wetsuits, no leashes, no sponsors, no stickers, and no judges. The competition would be held at Jeffreys Bay. The surf had to be 8 feet or over; that meant wintertime and cold water. The contest would be for the longest ride. The only judging would be somebody on the beach with a flag; they would plant a flag where you took off on the wave and then plant another flag where you ended up. The surfer who traveled the farthest distance would be the winner. Building on that article, Wes and his partners had written a movie script.

It was about three months before the shoot would start, so there wasn't a whole lot of time to design and build my board and cold-water outfit from concept to reality. I talked with Peggy and made sure our finances and schedules could handle the commitment. Then I started in on the board. My nephew had left a blank a couple years before that was made from century plant. It was irregular and tweaked, but it would have to do. I called him, and he said it was OK to use it.

I had never surfed Jeffreys Bay – I had only talked to people who had – but I knew that cold water and paddling speed, as well as my age, were going to be issues. I really wanted to build a short board, or at least something that worked like a short board, but being limited to a single fin and a 10-inch square tail made the board pretty interesting to design. I mucked around and thought about different designs and lengths. Finally, I settled on an 8'10" length, for no other reason than that my first real surfboard from Joe Quigg was an 8'10".

I drew an outline that looked reasonable for that tail width. I wanted a pointy nose to penetrate Jeffreys Bay's offshore winds. The wood was not as dense as balsa, so the board wasn't very sound structurally. Without glass on it, I could literally claw chunks out of it. I knew that in reality we would have to use leashes; otherwise, there would be no film, so I had to have a way to attach a leash. Besides having an attachment point for the leash, I also had to protect the rail from the leash, and I had to somehow affix a fin onto this mush. It was an interesting engineering exercise.

To solve those problems, I scarfed some denser balsawood around the fin area. Around the rails aft I inlaid bamboo; it is light and would keep the leash from cutting through the rail. I made a wooden fin box and jammed the fin in with newspaper, like we did back in the '50s.

Knowing Dora, he would have cheated. I didn't steal a credit card to get to South Africa, but I did use epoxy resin to saturate the wood to make it more cohesive, and I did make my fin out of birch plywood that had been glued together with a waterproof synthetic glue. Then I coated the board with a natural varnish.

I only had time to ride the board once before I left; a blown-out, knee- to waist-high day at Old Man's at San Onofre. Then I packed it up with a couple of conventional

The Aquatic Ape. *Robert Weaver*

boards and left for South Africa. Before I left, I went down to the thrift store to buy some wool sweaters – what we used before wetsuits – and cut the sleeves off. I used to surf Ventura Overhead and Rincon a lot, and a wool sweater was my winter outfit. This time I picked up a Scottish wool suit jacket at the thrift store, because I figured the Scots knew as much about cold as anybody. I brought it home and cut the buttons and sleeves off the jacket, and laced it on like a vest. I had a wool balaclava for head protection and a pair of wool pants that I cut off just below the knees. That was my uniform for riding Jeffreys Bay.

Wingnut and Marc Andreini were also invited, and we all met up in South Africa. Wingnut cheated; he wasn't a surfboard shaper, so he brought two balsa boards shaped by others. One board was shaped by Randy French with a 10-inch asymmetrical diagonal tail, instead of a square one. That was cheating big time.

Marc designed and shaped his own board. It was by far the most beautiful of the boards – a more traditional longboard style.

We met up at the house where we were to stay. The day we arrived, the surf was small. The locals showed us the best place to go out where there was a little sand and we could get our boards out through the surf. The rest of the point was all full-power, right onto the rocks. It was gnarly. The current was going down the beach as fast as you could run. That was all good advice, but after three days of travel, it was the next day before we decided to experiment with our wood boards. We got an hour or two in the water, and then the rest of the day was used getting our act together.

The next day, the surf was double to triple overhead and grinding a mile down the beach. I decided to paddle out, but our previous paddle-out spot was now the wrong place to paddle out. It was breaking 200 yards off the beach, top to bottom and sucking sand over the falls and with no lull in the waves. It ended up being a 45-minute paddle out, and I got hammered. Finally, I got a break between waves and I got out.

There was one other guy sitting outside, and he took off on a set wave. I tried for the second wave of the set but didn't paddle down the face far enough, and the offshore winds held me back. I floated down the face of the wave standing on my board and then get hammered by the lip all the way to the bottom. I climbed my leash back up to the surface just in time for the next wave to hammer me back down to the bottom. On the first wave, I hit with so much impact I put five fractures across the bottom of my board. That was my welcome to J Bay.

In the couple hours of being out there, I managed to get three or four waves. All the best surfers left over from the contest a week before knew this swell was coming, so they stuck around. Trying to get a wave in that crew was not easy. Getting back in was almost as tough as getting out. The waves were breaking full power 50 to 100 feet from exposed rock. You had to time the current and waves just right to get into this slot in through the rocks. If you missed you would be climbing over the rocks with whitewater bashing and crashing you.

After I got in, the group decided that this was the perfect day to shoot the film. We ate lunch, and then we suited up in our ridiculous costumes. Wingnut had brought a little leather vest, which was absolutely the wrong thing to wear. He looked like he was going to a gay bar. Marc had taken a Pendleton shirt and cut it off at his elbows and had a pair of wool shorts on, and that was his outfit. I looked like a *Waterworld* extra with my balaclava and my tweed Scottish suit jacket.

The locals showed us the tricky slot that was the go-out when the surf was this big. You had to jump into this thing when it was full of water and go left, then right, past the boils and rocks, and then you were paddling right into Supertubes. If you timed it right, you could paddle with the current in time to get out between the waves. Problem was, you couldn't see the swells coming from around the point. I figured the pros knew what they were doing, so I picked out two shortboarders that were getting ready to go out, and when they jumped in, so did I. There wasn't enough room in the slot for three people so I had looked to the right of the slot and scoped out a risky circuitous path through the boils and rocks. I somehow cleared the underwater rocks with my fin still on my board and paddled straight out into a set wave at Supertubes punching through the breaking lip barely in time to avoid certain disaster. I think when Wingnut and Mark saw how close I had come to not making it out, they stood on the beach for another 45 minutes waiting for a break in the waves to get out.

I paddled to the outside point where I'd ridden earlier and sat there waiting for a set to come through. One came, and Shaun Tomson, who I had been talking with while waiting, called me into a wave. I got a pretty good ride, made it out of this thing and started the long paddle back up. Meanwhile, Wingnut and Marc still hadn't made it off the beach yet.

About the time I got my second wave, they made it out. Some of the best surfers in the world were out there. There were five fins, '70s era twin-fin fish, exotic thrusters, longboards, and ev-

CLOCKWISE FROM TOP:
Up and riding: The board didn't work that bad.
Jack English

It was an interesting engineering project to make the right fin for a 10-inch squaretail, single fin. *Jeff Divine*

The rules specified that we couldn't use a leash, but I knew there wouldn't be a film without one. Here is what I came up with to accommodate the spirit of the contest, the realities of the project, and the strengths and weaknesses of the natural materials. *Jeff Divine*

ery kind of gun imaginable. There were all kinds of designs being ridden, and the pros were very interested in what we were doing. They let me have a couple waves, and on my last wave, I ended up just surfing into oblivion, riding from the outside point through Supertubes into Impossibles and wiping out past the slot to get in. With the size of the waves and the radical current there was no paddling back up the point, the only way in was through the exposed rock. I used my board as a battering ram and bounced up on the inside rock shelf. I came out bleeding head to foot. I was so stoked though, I couldn't stop grinning.

Wingnut got a pretty darn good ride. He had broken his longer board and so was riding the real cheater that Randy had made him. Under the rules, I beat both Wingnut and Marc. We had a great time: We surfed exotic places, the locals were friendly, and we did stupid stuff and got away with. It was like a 1950s surf trip.

The Stand-Up Revolution

I believe the stand-up revolution occurred because it's a faster, easier way to get around on a surfboard. You also have better vision because you are standing and the added benefit of eliminating the crucial step of getting from prone to upright on a board. The paddling advantage is similar to the reason longboards experienced a revival. Surfing is fun, and the more waves you ride, the more fun you have. Fun boards are popular.

There are some other obvious reasons that stand-up paddling is gaining so much popularity. You can paddle about anywhere there is water, and it's easy enough that beginners and intermediates can enjoy it right away. From a health standpoint, stand-up paddling is easy on your body, so you can spend more time doing it and get plenty of exercise. Your balance improves, and the view can't be beat. There are also many facets of interest, from racing to surfing, exercise to expedition; mostly it's just the sheer joy of being on the water.

The design challenge is interesting; the boards are everything you need to stand up on and everything you don't want riding a wave. It's similar to the problem that speed is no good unless you can control it. The one redeeming factor is the paddle. The paddle is not only your propeller, but it's an adjustable foil that can create lift as well as steer.

Designing a board to cruise on is relatively easy: Make it long, wide, and thick for stability. But the longer, wider, and thicker they are, the heavier and more expensive they get. At the other extreme, race boards tend to be longer, thicker, and more difficult to shape, and you try to keep them light, which takes more sophisticated and expensive materials and building techniques. Shapes for surfing are evolving similar to surfboards: There are big-wave guns, longboard styles, cruisers, funboards, fish, and shortboards. The caveat is that you have to make them stable enough to paddle standing up.

Stand-up paddling has some growing pains; its popularity has attracted a wide range of people and entrepreneurs, some of whom are not as educated in water safety and water etiquette as they should be. That has led to some safety and right-of-way issues. It's parallel to what occurred when snowboarding became popular and conflict developed between snowboarders and ski resorts and skiers. Snowboarders had an attitude; they dressed differently, they rode a different line than the skiers, they had a blind side because of their stance, and their equipment and skill level wasn't that great.

It took a few years to work through the problems – educating the players and making huge improvements in snowboard equipment and rider skill – but the conflict turned into respect that worked both ways. Snowboarders were riding the mountain like a wave, able to carve tracks that only the very best skiers could do. Skiers started crossing over to snowboarding, ski designers redesigned skis using snowboard design ideas like the deep side cut that changed skiing forever. With the new designs, skiers of average ability could carve turns like the snowboarders. Ski racers were running courses faster than ever. Snowboarding became accepted and skiing more exciting; the resorts that that had been dying because of lack of interest had a new generation of stoke.

I see a similar path for stand-ups and surfing. The players are more aware, the quality of equipment and skill of the paddlers has already improved, and the spin-off from what we learn will benefit all.

ABOVE: *Jeff Divine*

OPPOSITE PAGE: *Jim Coshland*

Flippy's Last Drop

Flippy Hoffman and I had a relationship that started in the early '50s and was based on a lot of common interests. It started with water being the main one. Besides being an excellent waterman, he was a very shrewd entrepreneur and businessman, which I wasn't. He had a great eye for art and creativity. I fancied myself as a creative sort, being a shaper and designer of boards and other watercraft. Seemed like we always had something to discuss or argue about. We traveled, dove, and surfed a lot together, and I helped him build his boats and shaped a lot of his boards.

When Peggy and I were still dating and both had full-time jobs, we had a trip planned for an upcoming Easter vacation. Just before our trip, Flippy called me and said, "You got to come and work. You got to finish my boat. You got to finish my deck."

I replied that Peggy and I were going on a trip, and I couldn't, but Peggy reminded me that he was my friend and I had to help him. So I spent Easter vacation working on his boat deck: grinding fiberglass, glassing, and then laying down the final nonskid surface on a big 12-foot by 12-foot plywood deck.

I told him what I charge an hour, and if he came and hung out that I would charge him a third more an hour, and if he came, hung out and made any suggestions, I would charge him double what I normally charge.

He couldn't help himself: He came and harassed me. That ritual went way back beyond the current boat I was working on. We built his first boat in his warehouse in Santa Ana, while his dad, Rube, was still alive and vitally involved in the business. Flippy had me grinding fiberglass – I was dressed in coveralls with taped wrists, ankles and neck, and with hood and mask on – with clouds of white death flying through the air. I was in a storage room with bolts and bolts of fabric for the business, Flippy was telling me, "Don't tell my

This is one of my favorite shots of Flippy. Baja. *Mickey Muñoz*

dad what you're doing." Meanwhile, Rube was standing in the doorway, shaking his head.

So there I was working on Easter vacation when I was supposed to be with Peggy, and Flippy was screaming at me, telling me how to do my job. I had just catalyzed a half gallon of resin with gray pigment. I was brushing out a pretty big deck, and it was a dance to get the resin on smoothly before it goes off. I was getting down to the short strokes, and Flippy was there, screaming at me about how I could do a better job.

I snapped. I said, "OK, Flippy," and I took the resin with the brush in it, threw it straight up in the air, walked out from under it and walked out. The bucket of resin came down and just splattered. As I walked away, I was just enough ahead of it that I got nothing on me, but it nailed Flippy and everything on the floor. It was a mess. He didn't talk to me for a week. Finally, I felt so bad I called him and apologized. That was what our relationship was like over the years: loving and hating each other.

Years ago, Walter Hoffman's wife, Trish, used to crochet bikinis for the girls. She got an order from some gay guy in Laguna for a bikini bottom and crocheted a bikini bottom for him, but the guy never picked it up. She knew only one person who would wear it, so she gave it to me.

I don't remember why I had the bikini with me, but Flippy and I were out at San Clemente Island diving. It was a Saturday afternoon with beautiful weather. We came around the corner into Pyramid Cove, and Flippy was driving the boat wearing a ratty tee shirt and his old shitty shorts covered with fish blood. The whole commercial fleet was in the anchorage, so Flippy was driving and giving each boat as we pass a "side-eye" plus a raised hand, pretending that we too were commercial. It wasn't too hard because his boat was kind of a spectacle – a power cat with four posts and a sun cover strung between them and mismatched outboards.

Meanwhile, I had slipped below and put this little bikini number on and come back up. Flippy was not one for "man hugs," but it was OK on the boat to hold onto one of the posts with one hand and have your other hand on the waist or shoulder of the person next to you so you didn't fall. I put my hand on his waist, while he and I talked, and I also started, "side-eyeing" and waving to the fleet. Flippy didn't realize I had on this scandalous little bikini. The commercial guys started to stare, laugh, and point. Finally, Flippy turns, sees my outfit, and says, "You bastard." He dove into the cabin and wouldn't come out until after I anchored and the sun went down.

He would always criticize me. "You can't surf. You can't learn to snowboard. What are you trying to do? You're too old to snowboard. You can't do that stand-up." I never took it personally. I would laugh and just do it anyway, and he loved it; he loved it that I did it despite what he said.

If you couldn't take abuse, you couldn't work for him; you couldn't take it personally – that was just his personality. I would go to where he worked and pick him up to go up to his boat and get him out of there to go adventuring. I would walk in there, and everybody would beg me, "Get him out of here. Get him out of here. God, we're so glad to see you, get him out of here."

But he had heart and everybody knew it. The people who worked for him, worked for him for 30 or 40 years. They knew that he was always fair in the long run. He'd scream about penny-pinching, but in the long run he would pay, and he would always pay right. He was honest. He was like a sea urchin: The spines could get you, but the insides were sweet and delicious.

This last time going to Mexico after he died was a little empty for me; I used to take a lot of photographs with Flippy in mind. He was always interested in what conditions were like on my trips or even on my surfs: "How were the conditions? Who was doing what? Did you go diving? Where did you surf? How big was the surf? How much wind was there? What was the temperature? What did my place look like?"

We would talk three, four times a week. If I went to the Channel Islands and he didn't, or I went surfing, wherever and whatever, I would always report the conditions and events.

The beginning of the end came with a diving accident out at San Clemente Island after he hurried to get in the water and didn't plug his buoyancy compensator in properly. In the ensuing frustration to fix it while keeping his gear together, he got so pissed off that he had a small stroke, enough that his left side went numb. He lost his mobility and drifted to the surface. One of his diving partners saw him, pulled him back to the boat and called the Coast Guard.

He came out of treatment slightly impaired but was determined to surf, though he couldn't stand up on the board. He still went out and paddled into waves, and he was fearless in big waves. He rode Avalanche at 30 feet and fell off his Jet Ski and somehow got in. The stroke was a big blow to him and a real low point. Then it seemed like he started progressing and getting a little better, getting a little more movement and strength.

A couple of years ago, he started having a tough time breathing. It turned out he had pulmonary fibrosis. It might have been a combination of smoking and so much scuba diving, breathing the dry air. His breathing got harder and harder, and he started

using oxygen. He had to figure out how to drag his oxygen tank around when he traveled. He would fly without oxygen, and then he'd be really screwed up for a few days.

Two winters back in Hawai'i, he rode his Jet Ski out in front of his house with nobody else with him. The steering broke, he fell off and couldn't get back on, and he ended up hanging on to the side of the ski drifting in through pretty big surf and washing up on the beach. They got him to the hospital, and they didn't know how to treat him. He had his son bust him out of there and bring him back to the mainland.

A day later, the doctor from Hawai'i called his brother Walter and asked, "Have you seen Flippy? Do you know where Flippy is? He's supposed to be in the hospital."

Walter replied, "He's right next door."

The doctor said, "You're kidding? He's still supposed to be in the hospital; he can't fly."

That episode triggered even more problems. Eventually, it got to the point where he couldn't even use a walker. The last six or eight months, he had a full-time nurse to help take care of him. Even then, it was hard to believe that he wouldn't be there the next day. We would take him out on his boat at least once a week; get him down the ramp in the wheelchair and lift him up on his boat and take him out cruising.

I visited him the day before he went into the hospital the last time, and he was complaining about his shoulder; he thought he had pulled a muscle or something. The next day Flippy and his girlfriend Susie had invited some friends over to dinner. Flippy was real anxious during that day, and after the guests left, he was up most of the night. About 3:00 in the morning, the nurse called the paramedics.

At the hospital, they induced a coma because Flippy had given instructions to go to extreme measures to keep him alive as long as his mind was there. One of his big missions in his last year or two was working on his will. He was in the induced coma for 10 days. When his test results got to a reasonable level, they brought him out of the coma.

He woke up and was fully cognizant. When they told him he had been under for 10 days, he was shocked, and I think he realized then that there's no way he was going to go back

TOP TO BOTTOM:
Flippy waxes up a board for a go-out at San Clemente Island. *Mickey Muñoz*

Building one of Flippy's boats at Poche. *Mickey Muñoz*

We took a 28-foot Wilson all the way down the Pacific coast to Cabo. We surfed, dove, and fished in just about every good spot. We had a blast. Dick Beecham owned the boat, and the crew consisted of his cousin, me, and Flippy. *Mickey Muñoz*

home better than when he left – more than likely, he would go home much worse. So he just said that was it; he was done. He wanted to die that night. Two or three different doctors came in and questioned him, and he gave each the same story.

One of Flippy's mantras was, "Pay extra for the morphine drip." They were maxing him out on whatever the law would allow for morphine, and they started to pull him off the life support – the feeding tubes and oxygen. The family had been called, and he said his good-byes.

I got in from surfing late, and Peggy told me I had to go to the hospital; Flippy wanted to die tonight. Peggy gave me a little abalone shell to take and said that he would love it. I got there, and the family was standing around his bed. Carl Iverson and Warren Goff were there, longtime friends who had done tons of island trips with Flippy on his boat.

At an opportune time when there was a lull in the action and I was standing next to the bed, I grabbed his hand. He started to pull his hand away, but then let it lie. I said to him, "You know I love you, and I'm going to miss you." I was in tears.

Before I left around 9:00 I looked at the monitor by his bed and saw that his blood pressure was at a reasonable level as was his blood oxygen. I left thinking his body is so tough, even if his mind says, "I want out of here," his body wasn't going to let him go.

At 3:30 am his heart stopped. I woke up at a quarter to 4:00 sobbing. I couldn't figure out why, and then I started to think about him. So that was it. Flippy's last drop was a 6-footer.

Right on course. *Mickey Muñoz*

The Mongoose Cup

The City of Dana Point approached the Doheny long-board club and asked if they would be interested in putting on an event in conjunction with the city's weeklong whale festival to fill a hole in their itinerary. The Doheny longboard club came to me and asked me if they could use my name for the event. I thought about it and said yes, if it was about education and safety for stand-up paddlers.

Back when they asked me, stand-up surfing and paddling was growing rapidly in numbers and popularity, and there was a lot of conflict between conventional surfers and stand-up paddle surfers in the lineup, as well as conflict between boaters and stand-up paddlers in the harbor. There were a lot of naive paddlers, boaters, and surfers out there.

At the same time the Coast Guard had recently defined stand-up paddleboards as vessels and required them to carry all the safety gear that they require on a rowboat or kayak: a PFD and a whistle or air horn. The Coast Guard requirement was that you have a PFD with you – the Coast Guard suggests you wear it, but they can't make you wear it. Beginning paddlers would naively think that because they had a PFD with them that they were safe. But if they fell off their board and there was any wind or wave action that moved the board away or they couldn't get back to their board for some reason, that PFD wouldn't do them any good at all.

We came up with a better idea - a surfboard leash that attaches to way more flotation than a PFD. Of course the Coast Guard can't sanction leashes because they haven't tested them. Most of the municipalities, state, cities, and counties used the Coast Guard ruling to base their own laws on, which has led to confusion, especially in the surf zone. The Coast Guard defines stand-up boards as "swimming aids" in the surf zone, which changes the rules.

Technically I don't think stand-ups can be kept out of an area that is surfed, but I do believe that it should be discretionary. Surf spots like San Onofre, that have multiple breaks have segregated stand-ups and kayaks from a couple of their main surf breaks. I am not advocating segregation, but in the case of San Onofre, it has worked well. The main breaks are already crowded with conventional surfers, there are plenty of waves at the other breaks to go around, so there is a lot less friction and a lot more waves to ride.

Eventually it will work itself out like snowboarding and skiing did. There are waves more appropriate for shortboards, waves for longboarding, and waves for paddle surfing; some overlap and are good for all types of surfing. Surfing is definitely competitive at major breaks, the good surfers are going to get their waves no matter what boards they are riding, and they don't leave a lot waves for the pack. If you are surfing with proper etiquette and you're not getting waves, you're either on the wrong equipment or at the wrong break.

The original Mongoose Cup was set up as a clinic that emphasized safety and etiquette and tried to help educate about the PFD issue. The harbor department was simpatico and wanted to help rather than write tickets, so they became part of the educational process.

When you rent a Jet Ski or a stand-up board, or any type of sports equipment, there is always liability involved. The back of the rental form lists the rules and regulations and the liability that you are signing off to and will adhere to. Everybody's so excited about getting in the water that they hardly read it; as a result, they don't really know the rules.

Self-portrait at Dog Patch. *Mickey Muñoz*

We wanted to change that. We simplified the rules and etiquette into bullet points and, with the help of the harbor department, came up with a decal that simplified the etiquette of the surf lineup and the rules of the waterways into a form that was easy to understand and remember. Also on the decal was a map of the harbor showing the beginning and intermediate zones, the traffic circulation, and the restricted places where the Harbor Patrol didn't want people going – like around the powerboat launch ramp. This decal could then be placed at stand-up and kayak rental shops, launch areas, and on the boards themselves.

We held the Mongoose Cup, at Baby Beach. We distributed the decals and put up the signs and went over the rules and etiquette. We encouraged boaters to get involved because a lot of them were just as naive as the paddlers. It turned out that the boaters got so involved that they started paddling themselves

because it was a healthy way to see the harbor, and it was easy to store the boards on their boats. A lot of the boaters in our harbor have become stand-up paddlers because of these events.

We wanted the Mongoose Cup to be family oriented and not intimidating to those not familiar with the race scene; we didn't want only racers to show up. We started off with the safety and etiquette seminar; then we had a fun paddle around the island in the harbor. We had safety paddlers who were well-known stand-up paddlers in the area. They helped the beginners and intermediates with their paddle stroke and technique, and they gave advice on board and paddle designs. The paddle was just to get a bunch of people – paddlers, boaters, beginners, experts – to paddle together and share some knowledge.

Then we had a barbeque lunch, and in the afternoon we had relay races. The relay teams consisted of four paddlers with at least one senior, one junior, and one woman. It was a fun

way to get a little competition going and work some more on the skills that had been shared on the group paddle. And it was spectator friendly.

It worked out great: The city loved it. In fact, they came back and said they wanted to give us the whole day and the whole beach the next year. They've really encouraged this event.

The next year still emphasized safety and etiquette but had a more formal clinic feel. We had experts teach racers how to turn around race marks and how to refine their paddle technique. We also had somebody give advice on board and paddle choices and board first aid. We had a class on what stretches to do before and after paddling and on nutrition. We also had board manufacturers there giving demos of their equipment and paddles. To make the racing even less intimidating – the year before there were some stacked relay teams that were out for blood – we drew names for the teams out of a hat: "the luck

of the draw relay race." It didn't matter whether you won or lost, only how much fun you had. At the end of the event, we did a plastic pickup, a trash sweep of the harbor.

The Mongoose Cup was and is about educating: We're resolving some of the conflict in our particular area, and hopefully, that will spread to other places.

ABOVE:
Gidget and me going tandem. *Mickey Muñoz Collection*

OPPOSITE PAGE:
The first prototype of my 12'6" Water Rider: a hybrid paddle-anywhere, pack-your-gear-on-top, surf-anyplace-from-ankle-snappers-to-as-big-as-you-dare-take-off-on board. *Lucia Griggs*

Acknowledgments

Thanks first to Yvon who approached me with the idea to write a book. And then to all the book team at Patagonia who really did the work: John Dutton, the word editor, who is simpatico, he gets me; Jennifer Sullivan, who put all the players together and kept us moving forward; Peter McBride, for the book design; and all the behind the scenes staff. I am honored and privileged, thank you!

Patagonia didn't do all the work: My friend Steve Pezman sat through hours of *blah*, *blah*, trying to draw the best from me. Jeff Divine heroically carried boxes containing thousands and thousands of slides from my house to glean out a few of the better ones. I am a pack rat, I don't throw anything away, and that includes photos good and bad. He never got to the prints, or the couple hundred thousand digitals, oh well, next time!

To Peggy – my love, wife, and friend – who has never lost the passion for life she had when we first met, hooting, laughing, and holding her "mud," when adventure at times went bad: I love you darling!

To my son, Miguel, and daughter, Malia, who thrived despite my youthful foibles, I am so proud of both of you – love, Dad.

This book has been an interesting process; fun, educational, introspective, but also frustrating for all the material that I had to leave out due to time and space constraints. When Yvon and I talked about doing the book he gave me free rein to shape it anyway I wanted. There were some caveats though: a limit in size, number of pages, photographs, and words.

This gave me the parameters of the blank. The shape can change with your mood, how the light is, a missed cut with the planer, a different stroke with the sanding block, how that last wave you rode felt; any or all of these can change your perception and ideas. The book has morphed through different shapes, but the goal has remained the same: I wanted the book to be about all my friends, family and loves, all the waves, stories, the adventure, passion, and art; all the stuff that has shaped my life.

To my family and friends, and all the people I have met: Thank you for being the shapers, I am a very lucky surfin' pup!

Peggy and me in Baja. *Mickey Muñoz Collection*